THE WORKING MOTHER'S GUIDE TO SANITY

ELSA HOUTZ

CHRIST UNITED METHODIST CHURCH
4488 POPLAR AVENUE
MEMPHIS, TENNESSEE 38117

HARVEST HOUSE PUBLISHERS
Eugene, Oregon 97402

THE WORKING MOTHER'S GUIDE TO SANITY

Copyright © 1989 by Harvest House Publishers
Eugene, Oregon 97402

Library of Congress Cataloging-in-Publication Data

Houtz, Elsa, 1950-
    The working mother's guide to sanity.

        1. Working mothers—Psychology.   2. Working mothers—
Religious life.   I. Title.
HQ759.48.H68   1989   306.8′743   88-32050
ISBN 0-89081-744-8

Printed in the United States of America.

To the glory of God
and
To Mike and Matthew, with love

Contents

We're in This Together

When I first told my husband I was writing a book called *The Working Mother's Guide to Sanity*, he jokingly said, "Since when do *you* know anything about sanity?"

Funny guy.

*   *   *

Whenever I talk with other working mothers, I'm amazed at the commonality of our needs, our frustrations, our joys, and our dilemmas. It feels so good to know I'm not the only one whose house is overrun by unmatched socks or who finds that closing the curtains is a lot easier than washing the windows when company's coming. If nothing else, I hope this book will convince you that you are not alone, that there are working mothers everywhere struggling with the same things you struggle with: too much to do and too little time; guilt when you can't be in two (or three or four) places at once; pressure to be all things to all people; and the need to achieve some degree of balance between the numerous demands in your life.

You'll meet many of those working mothers—along with an assortment of other interesting people—in this book. Some people are identified by their real names, and others, out of respect for their privacy, aren't. I have quoted some of them verbatim and paraphrased the comments of others. But they are all very real. You will read about their experiences and, I hope, identify with their thoughts and feelings. I hope you will recognize their dilemmas as some of your own and say, "Yes! I know exactly how she feels!" and join me as we look for solutions. We will explore some different angles for looking at circumstances, and some ways to make positive changes in our day-to-day living; but we will also look at the deepest, most fundamental issues—the ones we grapple with late at night when the TV is off and the house is quiet. And we will reaffirm the good things in our lives and the good things about ourselves.

Not everyone has the fortitude to do what we are doing. It isn't easy. Some of the time it isn't even fun. But it's important. And its rewards are far beyond measure.

So we will forge ahead, carving out a place in history and culture for the phenomenon known to sociologists as the working mother. But let's not go it alone. We're in this together. Let's support and encourage each other. Let's acknowledge that we don't have all the answers, but we're doing the very best we can.

On the whole, we're doing a pretty good job.

Happy reading.

1 WORKING MOTHER 101

Course #101: "How to Be a Working Mother"

Prerequisites: Time Management I, II, and III; Juggling; Economics; History of the Universe; Advanced Trivia; Child Psychology; Adolescent Psychology; Adult Psychology; Abnormal Psychology; Logic; Argumentation and Debate; Business Administration; Food Science; Exotic Small Pets.

Course Description: An overview of the skills and training required for successful performance of the dual role of the mother who is also employed outside the home. Will examine such topics as: why dirty clothes always outnumber clean ones; the historical conflict between children and soap; how to avoid scheduling important meetings at work on the days you have peanut butter on your blouse; how to sound professional when answering telephone calls that begin, "Mom, you know that lizard I had?"

Okay, time for a pop quiz. Let's see how much you really know about being a working mother. Selecting one or more adjectives from the list provided, fill in the blank below:

"Being a working mother is a _____ job."

character-building	heartrending
colorful	horrifying
debilitating	intense
demanding	imaginative
dirty	impressive
disturbing	mind-boggling
exasperating	never-ending
excruciating	overwhelming
exhausting	rewarding
exhilarating	satisfying
fun	underpaid
frantic	underappreciated
frazzling	underestimated
fulfilling	varied
ghastly	victorious
gargantuan	wearying
harrowing	weird
healthful	wonderful
important	zesty

Whatever else it is, being a working mother is a difficult job (which wasn't on the list—who wrote this quiz, anyway?). It's doling out discipline and then wondering whether you have done the right thing; it's providing vast amounts of love, support, and encouragement, even when you don't feel like you have any to give; it's doing chores at 10 P.M. simply because they're there. It's watching a two-hour Little League game while the list of other things you need to be doing in your off-work time grows longer and longer.

That's why the expression "working mother" is so odd. Being a mother is work, period. It's happy work, sad work, satisfying work, exasperating work, tiring work, energizing work—but it's definitely work.

Some of us, though, for whatever reason, have another

job besides being a mother. We work in offices or factories or schools or stores for 30 or 40 hours a week, and the statisticians classify us as having full-time jobs.

They're wrong, of course. We have *two* full-time jobs.

Of the two, the one for which we receive a paycheck is probably the easier one. The rules are pretty clear. There's someone there to tell us how to do the job. We know what time to show up and when to go home. When we make a mistake, we find out right away, and there are ways of gauging how well we're doing; we don't have to wait 15 years to find out whether we did a good job or not. Either we get a raise or we don't. Either the contract is renewed or it isn't. Either our annual review is positive or it's not. Pretty simple compared to motherhood, isn't it?

Where do we learn how to be good mothers? Mostly from our own mothers, who, in all honesty, probably didn't know much more about the job than we do. We can learn how to be mothers from television and movies, too—but how do we decide who really has the right approach—Beaver Cleaver's mom, Elise Keaton of "Family Ties," or Cinderella's stepmother?

Part of the problem is that no one gives us a fixed set of guidelines for being good mothers. One expert says "Let your children express themselves freely so you won't hamper their self-actualization" while another says "Children *want* strict discipline; it gives them a sense of security—so let 'em have it!" Trends in parenting techniques, unfortunately, change almost as much as fashions do, so unless we make some firm decisions about the kind of mothers we want to be, we may find ourselves being strict one year and lenient the next! Our children will need a manual just to keep up with our changing rules.

On top of these fundamental difficulties of being a mother, those of us who also work outside the home carry around some added baggage. First, of course, are the basic logistical problems of fitting two full-time jobs into one day-to-day life. That involves finding the time and energy to give your best in both jobs, and still have enough left over to send birthday cards to your relatives, attend your friends' baby showers, get your hair cut, pay your bills, and change the cat's litter box.

As if that were not enough, we also have to cope with the headlines. You know the ones—you can pick up a major newspaper or magazine on any given day and find them. Do you recognize these?

"New Study Shows Children of Working Mothers Can't Read"

—————————

"Are Working Mothers Hurting Their Children?"

—————————

"Day-Care Scandal Rocks Nation"

—————————

"Toddler Cries, 'I Want Mommy to Come Home' "

Make you feel wonderful, don't they?

Another factor is that as mothers we are inclined to give out more than we get back. When a family member is ill, we do the caretaking, the soup-making, the blanket-tucking, the drugstore-running. But when we get sick, who does it for us? When a spouse or child is discouraged, hurting, frustrated, or just sad, we're there with support, encouragement, and—on rare occasions—words of wisdom. But when our own days are dreary, who is there for us?

To top it all off, there is the simple historical fact that no generation before ours has ever tried this. We can't look to history to find out how women in the past handled the "working mother" role, because it's a new societal phenomenon. We are the first, the pioneers, and charting new territories can be tough.

*   *   *

The day I ordered the cake for my son's ninth birthday, I learned that my own approach to being a working mother had gotten out of hand.

I wanted a specially-made cake, one with a baseball player on it, since my son likes baseball. It was a Tuesday evening, and his birthday was Saturday. I was patting myself on the back for planning ahead. My usual style would be to rush to the bakery the night before and take whatever cake they had on hand, even if it said "Good Luck in Your Retirement."

I had spent the last few days making detailed plans for the birthday party; buying matching paper plates, cups, and napkins; dreaming up games that could be played in our limited yard; and in general doing a very fine all-out, traditional-mother birthday-planning job. All this was done, of course, in the spaces between nine-hour days at the office and the usual roster of household chores. I was determined to be living proof that a working mother could still put on a bang-up birthday party.

So there I was, standing at the bakery counter while a young girl in a crisp uniform searched through her book of cake designs for a baseball figure. "I thought I saw one in here," she said. Then "Right. Here it is."

It was perfect—a batter in a blue-and-white uniform with a red cap. I was delighted. One more mission accomplished.

"Great!" I told the girl, and she began to write up the order. She asked me how big a cake I wanted, and what flavor, and what color icing, and told me how much it would cost.

Everything was fine until she said, "Now, when did you want to pick it up?"

Pick it up? I hadn't figured that into my schedule. (The store was ten minutes from my house, so we were talking about a 20-minute task.)

Something in my brain shorted out. The computer

in my mind flashed DISK FULL...INSUFFICIENT MEMORY...ERROR...ERROR....

I had plotted every moment of my life between Tuesday and Saturday, calculating exactly how everything had to fit together so that I would be ready by the time the party was to begin. I figured out what things I needed to get done on my lunch hour and what I could do after work.

I hadn't allowed the 20 minutes for picking up the cake. I hadn't even thought about picking up the cake. All the careful planning, the errand-running, the careful scheduling of the last few days was crumbling before my very eyes. I wanted to cry. My husband had to work all Saturday morning, then come home and set up the porch and the yard for the party, so he wasn't going to have a spare 20 minutes either.

What was I going to do? Picking up the cake would throw off my whole schedule! It would jeopardize the whole project! There was no place to fit it in! It was impossible! *I couldn't pick up the cake!*

The bakery clerk waited patiently. I stood there at the bakery counter, teary-eyed, totally overwhelmed, totally incapable of answering her question, wondering if that's what it felt like to have a nervous breakdown. At a bakery counter. How humiliating.

Finally, as mothers do, I rallied. I managed to say, "Saturday morning."

But there was more.

"What time?" she asked.

Am I going to live through this? I wondered.

"Ten," I said. "Ten in the morning."

"Okay," she said cheerfully. "See you then." She handed me the receipt for the order, and I raced out of the store.

On the way home, I obediently heeded a stern voice inside me that said, "Get a grip on yourself. What's the big deal about a 20-minute trip to pick up the cake?"

Then a nurturing voice took over. "You're probably just overtired. You'll feel better about things tomorrow."

They were both right, I told myself. But deep down, I knew something was wrong, something that didn't have anything to do with the birthday cake. Something was wrong with the way I was living my life, with the mother-image I was trying to live up to, with the roles I was trying to play.

Once again, as mothers do, I rallied. I completed all the arrangements for the party, picked up the cake Saturday morning, and Saturday afternoon was the proud hostess of a very successful birthday party.

The following Monday, however, I didn't go to work. Nor the following Tuesday, nor any day that week. I told my office that I was sick and not to call me. I even told my friends not to call me—and when the phone did ring, I didn't answer it. For most of the next five days I lay on the sofa in my family room, under the gold-colored Indian blanket from my mother's house, feeling infinitely alone, trying to figure out what I was doing wrong.

I had it all—job, home, family—so why did I feel like I was losing my mind? I was an intelligent, capable person, a successful executive who managed a large department efficiently. Why couldn't I manage my life better? Everything in my world was nice—nice house, nice child, nice husband, nice job, nice friends—but something inside me was not nice at all. Inside I was lonely, bruised, and hurting. I promised myself that before the week was out I would make some changes in the way I treated myself.

*   *   *

As a working mother, have you had a "birthday cake" experience—some task or event that was just one thing too many, a "last straw" that made you feel you couldn't cope any longer? Did it make you question whether you could—or even wanted to—continue juggling your many responsibilities? Did it make you wonder whether "having it all" was really having anything?

At times like that, we tend to feel that as working mothers we are always giving and seldom receiving. We stay up late making a bunny costume for the school Easter pageant, then feel crushed when our child's reaction is ho-hum. We make a half-dozen phone calls to line up a babysitter so we can put in some extra hours at work, and our boss doesn't even seem to notice. We stop at the grocery store on the way home from work, dash into the kitchen, and try out a new recipe for dinner—and the closest thing to a compliment we receive is "Gee, we've never had this before."

Even those of us who are married to helpful, supportive husbands (and I'm one of the lucky ones) aren't exempt from the rigors of working motherhood. Certainly a spouse who is willing to share the household and parenting responsibilities is a blessing to be cherished; still, the problems of guilt, overcommitment, role confusion, setting priorities, and sorting out expectations remain for the married woman as well as the single mother. When it comes to marital status, the challenge of working motherhood is an equal opportunity employer!

We work. We try our best to be good mothers. We nurture. We support. We meet other people's needs. And amid all the doing and going and being and pleasing and running, we seldom find ways to refresh our own spirits, to restore our own self-esteem, to acknowledge our own value as persons—as *persons*, not just as employees or mothers or some other role we play. Finding those ways to reaffirm ourselves is, I believe, a vital part of maintaining equilibrium and perspective in our lives. It's the key to staying sane in the crazy world of the working mother.

2 WHOSE SIDE ARE YOU ON?

Score: Working Mother—0;
        Everyone Else—1275

As a working mother, you really have two lives, your home life and your work life. Sometimes one is going well and the other isn't. When that happens, you can get away from the one that isn't going well and take refuge in the one that is, which is nice. Sometimes they're both going well; then you're on top of the world.

Sometimes neither is going well. That's when you're really in trouble.

—Benita

So much in our culture tells us to look outside ourselves for reassurance and reinforcement, both at home and at work. We look around us for ways to measure our own self-worth. We need things to go well at work and at home in order to feel good about ourselves and to feel positive about our lives. We want our superiors at work to recognize our contributions. We want our family life to be harmonious and satisfying. We want someone to say in some way, "I appreciate you." We need "strokes" from our environment in order to feel good about ourselves.

The rewards of the working world can be very, very enticing. The perks, the strokes, the recognition, and the paycheck can all be awfully appealing, especially on a day when your 13-year-old daughter says she hates you, your dog has to go to the veterinarian, and the plumber has had the water in your house turned off for two days. Motherhood is not an easy job; in fact, if you're like me, your job outside the home is probably infinitely easier and more manageable than your job at home.

As a result, we working mothers often face the temptation to invest ourselves more heavily in our job role or in social or civic activities simply because the rewards are more apparent and more immediate. A daily battle of wills with a teenager and mopping up after the plumber can make life on the job look downright glamorous while life at home seems frustrating and thankless. The temptation exists to invest more and more of our time, energy and talent in our jobs, which leaves less and less for other aspects of our lives.

As Benita says, when we aren't getting strokes from our home life, sometimes we can get them at work, or vice versa. But sometimes, instead of positive reinforcement and encouragement, all we get at work *or* at home is discouragement and conflict. We work for weeks on an important project, only to have the boss reject it. A coworker seems to take pleasure in criticizing us in front of other people. Our families ignore the hundreds of little tasks we do every day to keep the household afloat. Our children go to battle with us over the decisions we make for their own welfare. Nothing, *nothing* is going right. Our self-esteem plummets. We conclude that we must not be very worthwhile people because all the things we measure ourselves against are coming up negative.

That's the risk inherent in letting our self-worth be determined by the impermanent, arbitrary measures that surround us. If we assess our self-worth using measures like our boss' praise, our family's reaction to our Chicken à la Francais, the size of our paycheck, or the prestige of our neighborhood, we're doomed to ride a roller coaster.

If, on the other hand, we simply accept that we are valuable because God created us, then our self-worth is assured forever. Our value as persons isn't affected by what we do or don't achieve, by the way others feel about us, or by any changes that occur in our external circumstances.

> God created man in his own image; in the
> image of God he created him"
> (Genesis 1:27).

Would God create a being like Himself, and then not continue to cherish him, to be interested in his welfare, and to care what happened to him? The Bible says He wouldn't. "From heaven the Lord looks down and sees all mankind; from his dwelling place he watches all who live on earth—he who forms the hearts of all, who considers everything they do" (Psalm 33:13-15).

Try this: The next time you feel like you are in a nothing-but-nothing-is-going-right period and your self-esteem is in the basement, take a moment to reflect on the fact that you are a unique individual, lovingly created by God to be the person only you can be. Whatever happens in your world, nothing can change your inherent preciousness in God's sight.

Grab hold of the assurance that your real value does not come from what you do or don't do. It's not tied to being a good typist, a creative cook, an efficient home manager, or a model employee, but to the fact that God created you and cares about you. Armed with that knowledge, dive into the fray and see what happens!

The Woman in the Mirror: Friend or Foe?

If you had a friend who treated you the way you treat yourself, how long would you stay friends?
—Dr. John E. Anderson
President, Center for
Sports Psychology
Colorado Springs, Colorado

The next time you are by yourself—driving to work, standing at the sink, sitting in your office—listen to the way you talk to yourself. Do you hear yourself saying things like:

- "You did a great job on that report you turned in to the boss today. You should be proud of your good work."

- "You're a real show-stopper in that outfit. You'll knock 'em dead today!"

- "It's amazing that you were able to get all the laundry washed, dried, and put away in one evening, considering all the other things you had to get done at the same time."

- "I don't know how you managed to pick up all the supplies for Tim's Cub Scout meeting, but you did it. Way to go!"

- "You were so patient with Carrie when she was crying at dinner. Knowing how tired you were yourself, I'm proud of you."

Be honest, now. Are those the kind of things you say to yourself? Or do these quotes sound a little more familiar?

- "You dingbat. If you managed your time better you wouldn't be rushing around trying to finish that report."

- "Why didn't you start the laundry yesterday, like you planned to, so you would have time to go grocery shopping tonight? You're such a procrastinator!"

- "Timmy's clothes look like he slept in them. Why didn't you iron them?"

- "That outfit makes you look fat. But then, you *are* ten pounds overweight."

- "You idiot! Don't you remember the boss telling you she had a meeting Wednesday afternoon and not to schedule any appointments then? I can't believe you have such a bad memory."

Let's face it. We don't treat ourselves very well. We nag. We gripe. We find fault. We say things to ourselves we would never dream of saying to anyone else. We are so busy being loving and supportive to other people that we forget to give ourselves the same attention.

No person in history ever understood our needs as human beings better than Jesus. He was not only a human being like us, but He also had the insight and the wisdom of God. He knew and preached about what it takes for us to live happy, satisfying, meaningful lives. And one of the things He said was "Love your neighbor as yourself" (Matthew 22:39). Could He possibly have meant that we were to be hypercritical, negative, harsh, and unkind to other people? Of course not! He assumed that we cherished ourselves, cared lovingly for ourselves, gave ourselves the best treatment we could possibly give.

That's the kind of loving care He asks us to give other people.

Yet the reality of our lives as working mothers is that often we are so busy giving all our loving care away that we don't save any for ourselves. Instead, we abuse ourselves by demanding impossibly high standards and then being critical when they aren't met.

> *Do you not know that your body is a temple of the Holy Spirit, who is in you, whom you have received from God? You are not your own; you were bought at a price (1 Corinthians 6:19,20).*

God has an investment in each of us. Not only did He create us, but then He sent His only Son to show us how to live, and His Son died doing that. We are "not our own"; we are simply the stewards of the lives He has chosen to give us. Think what a change we can make if we treat ourselves with the tender, loving care worthy of His investment!

Try this: Tune in to your conversations with yourself. Jot down some of the things you hear yourself saying. See if you can keep a log or a diary of them for a day or more. Then review what you have written. See how many of the statements reflect tender, loving care and how many sound like Cinderella's wicked stepmother. Are you a friend or foe to yourself?

Now set a goal to make a certain number of positive, reinforcing statements to yourself tomorrow. Dr. Anderson (quoted earlier) suggests praising yourself for what he calls "little wins." Compliment yourself on the way you handle a certain situation or on finishing a simple task. Express appreciation to yourself for something you have done, however small. Think of the things you would

like a good friend to say, and say them to yourself.
Keep score. Practice. And praise yourself for accomplishing your goal!

> *An anxious heart weighs a man down, but a*
> *kind word cheers him up (Proverbs 12:25).*

Let that "kind word" be your gift to yourself.

3 THE THREE G'S: GUILT, GUILT, AND GUILT

I-Should-Be-Doing-Something-Else Guilt

When Kathy started running a few years ago, she just did it because she wanted to get some exercise and take off some extra pounds. She had a few friends who were serious runners who would run six or seven miles before they went to work in the morning, but she didn't have any plans that ambitious.

Before long, though, Kathy began to find that running did a lot more for her than just burning off calories. The exercise itself made her feel great. She felt healthier and more energetic, and was happy to notice that her clothes fit a little better. Someone at work even commented that she was looking especially trim lately.

Kathy liked both the early-morning run, when the air was fresh and the sun was just coming up, and the evening run, when she could feel the day's accumulated stress draining off with each step. She enjoyed the sense of accomplishment she felt each time she increased her distance, knowing she had built up greater endurance and strength.

Another benefit was that she made some new friends. She discovered some other women in her neighborhood

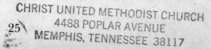

and at work who were runners, and often arranged to run with one or more of them. Some of them had even entered competitive "runs."

Eventually her friends talked Kathy into entering a run herself. It was just a short one, sponsored by a local runners' club, but entering it was an exciting milestone for Kathy. She didn't win, but she finished, and she was ecstatic. "I can't believe I did it!" she told her friends and family. She realized then that running had added a whole new dimension to her life, and she liked it.

However, in the best tradition of working-mother guilt, Kathy often wondered whether she was being selfish. After all, she was devoting several hours a week to her running instead of spending that time with her family or at home catching up on housework. Often the enjoyment and satisfaction she got out of her running was spoiled by the guilt she felt when she thought about all the other things she could be doing with those hours. Should she be baking cookies instead of trying to top her distance record?

Kathy's inner conflict is typical of the way working mothers feel when they do enjoyable things just for themselves. Into our so-called "leisure time"—the hours we aren't at work—we have to squeeze housework, shopping, chauffeuring, and other chores, then hope we have time left to maintain the quality of family life and social relationships that we want.

Somewhere we have picked up the idea that as working mothers we have to "make up" in some way for the time we spend at work. Because our jobs require us to be away from our families 40 or more hours a week, we feel that *all* our nonworking hours necessarily have to be spent doing home-and-family things. The result: When we have a chance to treat ourselves to something just for fun or just because it's satisfying to us, we feel guilty. This is a hard habit to break.

Guilt, in general, implies some act of wrongdoing, some crime. Yet even when we haven't done anything wrong, we feel guilty! How can it be wrong to treat yourself like a person, giving yourself equal time to do the things you enjoy? For some reason, when it comes to ourselves, our sense of justice breaks down.

When the Bible tells us to be just and merciful, I think that must apply to the way we treat ourselves, too—not just the way we treat others. I think God wants us to be as fair to ourselves as we try to be to other people.

—Rolle

According to the Bible, God wants justice in His world. If He wants you and me to be fair and merciful in our treatment of other people, it stands to reason that He also expects us to treat ourselves the same way. How about deciding right now to reduce the amount of I-Should-Be-Doing-Something-Else Guilt in your life?

The next time you have a chance to do something for yourself, to treat yourself just for fun (assuming it won't break the bank or disrupt your family relationships!), try this: Instead of mentally listing all the reasons why it wouldn't be fair to your family for you to do it, try saying, "I give my family and my job my very best efforts. I give my family my love, my support, and my caring. I give my job my skills in the best way I know how. Now I'm going to give myself something!"

Can you do it? Good for you.

But-I'm-Superhuman Guilt

Give yourself a break.
—My mother

One day when my mother was visiting me, she asked me if I had finished something she had asked me to do earlier. I was feeling very pressured at the time and was under a lot of stress at work and at home, and I really didn't want any more pressure. I snapped at her. "No," I said irritably, "I haven't done it! I've had about a million other things on my mind and I just haven't gotten around to it!"

I don't know about you, but I was taught from day one to be respectful toward my parents. I was horrified at the way I had spoken to my mother. But she wasn't. When I apologized later, she said, "Forget it. You're only human. Nobody but you expects you to be perfect, you know."

Her loving acceptance of my behavior was very reassuring and relieved the guilt I felt at having spoken unkindly to her. I realized later, though, how accurate her observation was. I do expect myself to be perfect, and when I'm not, I feel guilty.

If we confess our sins, he is faithful and just and will forgive us our sins... (1 John 1:9).

The Bible is filled with examples of forgiveness. God is always ready to forgive us; we have only to ask Him. If He can forgive us, surely we can forgive ourselves.

Similarly, Jesus asked us to forgive those who have wronged us, no matter how severe the wrong, and not just once—on "70 times seven" different occasions, if necessary.

When we forgive someone, we put their guilt behind

us, and we forget about it. We don't hold it against them or berate them over and over for what they have done. If they have been inconsiderate or forgetful or even unkind, we can simply accept it as human behavior, forgive and forget, and go on with the relationship.

But how do we treat *ourselves* when we make a mistake?

How many times have you poured But-I'm-Super-human Guilt on yourself? Like when you have just come home from work, fatigued and frazzled, and your two-year-old dumps his chocolate milk on the carpet? You lose your temper, you raise your voice, maybe even paddle him—and then mentally punish yourself the rest of the evening.

Or when your husband needs to wear his best suit for an important job interview and you said you would pick it up from the dry cleaners, but then the night before the interview you simply run out of time and when he reaches for it, it's not there?

None of us likes to let down those who depend on us. We hate to forget things that are important to our loved ones. It hurts us when we are harsh or unfair to our children. We could kick ourselves around the block when a family birthday or anniversary goes by and we haven't sent the card we meant to get. But it happens. It just happens. We're human. Our resources of patience, under-standing, energy, time, and ability to juggle our many responsibilities are limited, no matter how hard we try to stretch them to infinity.

Let's be more reasonable about our expectations of ourselves. If we know there's no way we can pick up that suit at the cleaners, let's say so and make some other arrangement. If we snap at a child or spouse, let's apolo-gize to them and then forgive ourselves, knowing it's bound to happen from time to time. If the house isn't straight out of *Better Homes and Gardens* all the time, so be it. Let's set some priorities we are comfortable with and stop criticizing ourselves for our failures.

Human beings make mistakes. Let's follow the example of forgiveness God gives us, not just in forgiving others but in forgiving ourselves.

> *Be kind and compassionate to one another,*
> *forgiving each other, just as in Christ God*
> *forgave you (Ephesians 4:32).*

No-Win Guilt

> Being a working mother is great as long as your
> kids stay healthy.
>
> —Dianne

Jill, a single mother who works full-time as a travel agent, told me a good story about No-Win Guilt. When her three-year-old daughter came down with the chicken pox, Jill naturally missed several days of work, since she had to stay home with her daughter.

When she returned to work the following week, one of her clients welcomed her back by saying, "Been having a little vacation, eh?"

"It was all I could do to keep from laughing," Jill told me later. "Imagine—taking care of a three-year-old with the chicken pox a vacation? Hardly! I was glad to get back to work!

"The whole time I was at home with Amy, I kept thinking I should be at work, and it made me feel guilty. After all, I wasn't sick myself. I could have been working. And yet, I had to stay with her; there just wasn't anyone else to take care of her. It's my job."

If we're at work, we feel guilty because we're not at home with our children. If we're at home with our children, we feel guilty because we're not at work. Talk about a no-win situation!

No-Win Guilt has the same earmarks as the two other kinds of guilt: treating ourselves unjustly and creating unrealistic expectations.

Realistically now, how can we be in two places at once? And how fair is it to let ourselves feel guilty because we're only one person, not a clone that can be duplicated as the situation demands?

Try this: Make a commitment to allow justice and forgiveness for yourself. Be alert to your own—and other people's—unrealistic expectations, and identify them as such. Try to be more tolerant of your own human mistakes, while you work at improving on your weaknesses. As you make efforts to be fair and understanding to others, extend that same generous spirit to yourself!

How's Your Guilt IQ?

How much of an expert on guilt are you?

Take this little quiz to find out. For each statement below, indicate whether it reflects:

#1: *I-Should-Be-Doing-Something-Else Guilt*
#2: *But-I'm-Superhuman Guilt*
#3: *No-Win Guilt*

After you've identified the kind of guilt, decide what *you* would do to deal with it.

———— "Why do the dirty socks always outnumber the clean ones, even the day after I do the laundry? My family never seems to have any clean clothes. Guess I should drop my aerobics class and do laundry on Tuesday nights instead."

_____ "If I don't go to the fifth-grade Christmas party, my son will be the only child there without a parent. His teacher might think he's an orphan."

_____ "I really should cook more. My kids will grow up thinking 'home-cooking' is food you pick up somewhere and take home to eat."

_____ "My son is talking out of turn at school and getting into trouble for it. I'll bet it's because I'm not with him enough and he wants more attention. It's my fault."

_____ "I let my son watch too much television just because it's so much easier for me to let him watch TV than to play games with him. He'll grow up to be a TV-crazed psychopath and it'll be my fault."

_____ "Just once, instead of coming home from work and having three or four people clamoring for my attention and wondering what's for dinner, I would like to come home to an empty house, put a frozen dinner in the oven, and read a book. Guess that's pretty selfish, huh?"

_____ "I really should keep the house cleaner."

_____ "I should be thankful for what I have and not complain just because I have so much to do. What a terrible, ungrateful person I am."

Congratulations! You receive a grade of A+ on this quiz—just for taking it. There are no right or wrong answers; it's just a way to get you thinking about the many kinds of "I'm guilty" statements we make, either verbally or in our heads.

Listen to yourself in the coming week, watching for "I'm guilty" statements—statements you actually express to someone else, or ones you make to yourself. When you hear one, decide what you want to do about it.

1) Determine whether you've really done anything wrong. As we discussed earlier, guilt implies wrongdoing.

Not long ago when I was in charge of a meeting at work, my watch stopped and the meeting ran a half-hour longer than it was supposed to. As a result, several of the people involved were late for another meeting right afterward, which was a major inconvenience to them and to the other people at that second meeting. I felt terribly guilty that I had let the meeting run over and caused them to be late.

Then, the more I thought about it, the more I could see how ridiculous it was to declare myself guilty of the "crime" of letting my watch stop. I hadn't done anything wrong—so I chose not to give in to guilt. (That was one of my more victorious encounters with guilt; I don't always win!)

2) Ask yourself whether you need to take some action to eliminate the cause of the guilt. Can you "fix" whatever it is you feel guilty about, or at least make a good-faith effort to improve or correct the situation? If that's practical and feasible, do it. If it will make you feel better to tell your toddler you're sorry for being cross and give him a hug, do it, rather than feeling guilty for the rest of the evening.

I don't know how often I have heard someone say, "So-and-so's father died a few weeks ago, and I haven't even sent her a card or called. I feel so guilty." Now that's a real case of wasted I-Should-Be-Doing-Something-Else Guilt. You feel like you should be sending the person a card or calling her on the phone, but you don't do it; instead, you just continue feeling guilty about it. So send the card! Just because it's a week or a month late doesn't mean the thought won't be appreciated. Your guilt over not doing it probably stems from knowing that the person needs your support and encouragement at this difficult time.

On the other hand, if you don't know the person that well and don't feel very motivated to make contact, don't. But make a choice! Doesn't that make more sense than carrying around an extra dose of guilt?

3) Make a decision not to just let guilt "ride." Don't carry it around. If there's no action you can take to remedy the situation, then simply drop the matter from your mental file. Guilt that we store away tends to build up and resurface later.

You might even try to picture in your mind some way of disposing of that particular "piece" of guilt. Imagine yourself rolling it into a ball and throwing it into the trash, or tying it to a helium balloon and letting it float away.

Like so many things, guilt will make us miserable if we let it. On the other hand, it can help us take constructive action. Guilt's only value lies in its ability to motivate us to act or cause us to reflect on some aspect of our thinking or behavior.

The better we understand God's concept of justice, the better we can distinguish between guilt that prompts positive change and guilt that simply leads us to needlessly punish ourselves.

4 YOU, ME, AND THEM
Which Is My Half?

"I give up," Wendy said. "No matter what I do, it's never right as far as Doris is concerned." (Doris was another woman who worked in the same department.)

"Any little thing I say, anything I do, just seems to make her angry or offend her," Wendy went on. "I honestly think she just plain doesn't like me."

Stressful relationships at work can not only make our workdays tense and fatiguing, but they can also make our lives at home miserable. Demanding bosses, uncooperative coworkers, and cantankerous customers can all take their toll on our nonworking hours. When we have spent a long day fighting frustration, anger, or hurt feelings, we are not likely to be loving and patient when we get home. A teenager's sarcastic remark at the dinner table or a toddler who resists going to bed can be the last straw. Having used up our day's quota of tolerance coping with a difficult person at work, we snap. All our pent-up anger and frustration from that difficult relationship gets dumped on an unsuspecting child or spouse. The household is disrupted. We feel guilty. An already rotten day gets worse.

Working mothers have enough on their minds without the added stress of an on-the-job relationship that's a constant battle. How do we cope with people who simply don't seem to want to get along with us?

Numerous books and articles have been written in recent years about personnel management, conflict resolution, and office relationships. But the best advice on the subject was actually written by the apostle Paul in about A.D. 57: "If it is possible," he wrote, "as far as it depends on you, live at peace with everyone" (Romans 12:18).

The wording of his advice is particularly interesting. "*If* it is possible." "*As far as* it depends on you."

The fact is that we control only half of any relationship in our lives. What we do with our half is up to us; what other people do with their half is up to them. When we are sure that we have done the very best we can with our half to make the relationship work, then we have done our part.

We cannot change other people, nor can we control or dictate what they do with their part of the relationship. If we constantly fight to change the way they handle it, we will only end up frustrated and hurt.

Wendy cannot change Doris' behavior. Until she accepts that, she will be on edge every time Doris is anywhere near her. She can expect to be filled with anxiety as long as she fights inwardly against something she simply cannot control.

On the other hand, Wendy can fully control how she handles her half of the relationship. While she can't change Doris' behavior, she can do things that may influence Doris to change it herself. Wendy can work hard to treat Doris with courtesy and consideration. She can try to make gestures of kindness and friendship, knowing that they may be rejected or rebuffed. But she will have done her part, having done everything possible to "live at peace" with Doris. How Doris responds is her responsibility.

> She's just really not my sort of person.
> —Jeanie

St. Francis of Assisi's ageless prayer applies perfectly to countless situations, and is especially pertinent to human relationships:

> God, grant me the serenity to accept the
> things I cannot change, the courage to
> change the things I can, and the wisdom to
> know the difference.

A Little Help from Our Friends

A working mother's life is a hodgepodge of relationships—good ones, bad ones, and neutral ones. Just as we can find ways to deal with the difficult ones to reduce the stress they cause, we can also work to make the most of the positive ones—the friendships that come our way. With a little work and a lot of TLC, our friendships can be among the greatest sources of warmth, joy, and encouragement in our hectic lives.

Today's self-help experts advise each of us to create a "support network" for ourselves—a circle of people we can count on to listen, to care, to understand, people whose advice and judgment we respect. In short, a circle of friends. But the important role of friendship in our lives is not a discovery of modern-day psychologists. The Bible, in both the Old and New Testaments, repeatedly acknowledges the value of friendship and the worth of friends. The expressions "close friend" and "closest friend" occur frequently in the Scriptures.

In our mobile society, often our family circle is far-flung throughout a city, a state, the country, or even the world. In addition, because the pace of change in our world is so rapid, those of us in the relatively new role of working mothers may feel separated by a generation gap from our mothers and other women of their generation. While they may give us love and support, they reared their children in a different world, and many of them are unfamiliar with the pressures that face today's working mother. We turn for understanding to other working mothers, drawing on our common experiences for encouragement and a sense of belonging.

Our friends fill an important gap in our lives, often providing the support we need in the absence of close family members. The Bible suggests that friends are sometimes even closer than blood relatives. It is not unusual for a person to have more in common with a friend than with a sibling whose life has followed a much different course.

> *There is a friend who sticks closer than a brother (Proverbs 18:24).*

In the absence of role models from the previous generation, we often turn to our fellow working mothers for advice and example. I couldn't begin to count all the times I have talked at great length with friends about the universal problems of rearing children, juggling schedules, dealing with guilt, and managing work and home. If I see someone else who seems to be handling a particular problem well, I don't hesitate to corner her and say, "Tell me how you do it!" (More often than not, though, she says something like, "Don't be fooled—I'm not as much in control as I appear. Inside, I'm a wreck!")

I was lamenting to one mother how I always seemed to be caught off-guard by school holidays—not the familiar ones like Thanksgiving and Christmas, but ones like Columbus Day or teachers' conference day. It always seemed like I never heard about them until the last minute. My son would say, "Mom, what am I doing on Friday?" And I would answer, "Going to school, aren't you?" And he would say, "No, there's no school." Then I would make frantic telephone calls for the next few days, trying to arrange day-care at the last minute.

"What I do," my friend said, "is this: As soon as I receive the school calendar for the year, I copy all the important dates and days off onto the wall calendar in my kitchen—so I always know when there's a school holiday coming up."

It was so simple that it was embarrassing!

When you get right down to it, we're all in the same boat; that's why it is natural—and important—for us to support one another, share ideas, and learn from each other's experiences. "Networking" is a valuable way of maintaining our equilibrium!

Friendship: Tonic for a Weary Spirit

It was a terrible week at the office. The phone, the paperwork, the squeeze of too little time for too much work, and the stress of dealing with other people's problems had left me exhausted, frustrated, and feeling very much at the end of my rope. I needed to talk to someone. I called Karen, who was a manager in another department, and said, "I need a friend. Can you have lunch with me?"

She willingly consented. I unloaded all my little gripes and aggravations that had piled up during the week and she listened, occasionally offering a suggestion or an insight. She commiserated with my frustrations and agreed wholeheartedly that I had every reason to feel the way I did. As she always does, she even made me laugh.

I felt better after our lunch together. I was glad I had called her and grateful to have such a loyal friend.

The pleasantness of one's friend springs from his earnest counsel (Proverbs 27:9).

Imagine how surprised I was the next day when I received a note from her that said, "Thanks for thinking of me when you needed a friend. I'm glad you called me. It makes me feel good that you thought of me. Love, Karen."

I thought Karen had done me a favor by letting me pour out my feelings to her. Yet she felt flattered that I turned to her when I was feeling in need of support.

Karen taught me that letting someone else be a friend to me is as important as being a friend to myself. By calling her when I needed a sympathetic ear, I let Karen know that I trusted her with my feelings and knew I could count on her to care about me. It made her feel good to know I had that much confidence in her friendship.

The Bible tells us it is more blessed to give than to receive. Sometimes, though, the best form of giving is graciously accepting the loving, caring gestures of other people. Our pride and our desire to appear self-sufficient can make this hard to do. When we put those feelings aside and simply receive with gratitude, we give other people a sense of being needed and appreciated. It is a rare privilege to be able to give and receive at the same time.

Jennifer and Sheryl had grown up together and been friends all through school. They moved to different states after graduating from high school, but they stayed in touch and often visited one another. Even though separated by distance, they still considered themselves "best friends."

When both women were in their mid-thirties, Sheryl

received a phone call one night from Jennifer's sister, saying that Jennifer had committed suicide the night before. Her suicide had been carefully planned, and she had left a note explaining that she just didn't want to go on living anymore. But she didn't really say why. Even her family wasn't sure what had caused her to make such a desperate choice.

Sobbing with grief and anger, Sheryl said, "Why didn't she tell me she was hurting? I would have done anything for her. I would have helped. How could she do this? How could anything be that bad, and she didn't even tell me?"

A friend loves at all times... (Proverbs 17:17).

Just as we trust our friends with our innermost feelings—from the most triumphant joy to the bleakest despair—we expect them to trust us, too. Sheryl's grief was made more painful by her feeling that Jennifer had somehow betrayed her and their friendship. When Jennifer had needed a friend the most, in the midst of depression and pain, she had not given Sheryl a chance to help. Sheryl felt that Jennifer had not trusted her to care enough or love enough in a real crisis. Besides the loss of a lifelong friend, that was what hurt the most.

Letting our friends know we have confidence in their love and concern for us is sometimes the best way of being a friend.

> I think the things that are important to your friends should be important to you, too.
>
> —Lona

The Bible also frequently refers to the role of friends in the celebration or the observation of important occasions—births, funerals, weddings, banquets. One of the ways we let our friends know how important they are to us is by including them in the events that are meaningful in our lives. We can invite friends to help celebrate a job promotion, ask them to attend a baptism or a family birthday celebration, or call them when we have a setback and need encouragement.

By the same token, we demonstrate friendship by participating in the bright moments—as well as the dark moments—of our friends' lives.

When my telephone rang one Saturday night last year, it was my friend Lynn, calling to tell me the husband of a mutual friend, Paula, had been killed in a car accident. Paula and I had worked together for several years and become close friends, although we had both changed jobs since then and hadn't seen one another in over a year.

I didn't know what I would say or do when I got there, but I knew I needed to go visit her at her parents' home that night, just to let her know I was there if she needed a friend. When I arrived, a tearful, shock-battered Paula hugged me and said, "I knew you'd come." I was touched to realize that even though we hadn't seen one another in a long time, she still knew I would care enough to share her grief.

The Risk Versus the Rewards

Recently our Sunday school class had a discussion on friendship. At the beginning of the class, we talked about ways friendships begin. What creates the initial attraction that makes us view another person as a potential friend? Some of the class' responses were "common interests"; "finding that the person is easy to talk to"; "similar situations—work, school, or having children who are about the same age or in the same activities"; "discovering that you feel the same way about a lot of things"; and "finding someone who's a good listener."

While "love at first sight" may make for romantic storytelling, friendship—like lasting love—is the result of a gradual process, one that is likely to begin with a circumstantial encounter.

> Friendship takes a lot of work. It's an investment.
>
> —Chuck

Does that mean we sit back and wait for friends to wander by chance into our lives? Is friendship a matter of rolling the proverbial dice and hoping that deep and satisfying relationships will come our way?

It doesn't have to be. Like so many things, the quality of friendships in our lives depends to a great extent on the investment and effort we put into building them—an effort that may even involve a risk of rejection. Often, simply being willing to take the first, risky step to launch a new friendship can make all the difference. It can be as simple as inviting a new coworker or a new neighbor to have a cup of coffee, but someone has to take the first step.

"I Never Seem to Have Any Time"

Try this: Sketch out your schedule for, say, the next three days. Draw a column for each day. Starting with the time you get up in the morning on the first day, write in and label time slots for all the things you need to do. Include the time it takes you to go to and from work, take children to and from school, etc. Try to give an accurate picture of your schedule. In any time blocks in which you don't have anything specific you need to do, write "free time."

> I don't think you set out to be friends with someone. I think it just happens. As you become better acquainted, you find you have more and more in common and enjoy being together.
>
> —Lee

If your schedule looks like a typical working mother's, you don't have many—if any—time blocks labeled "free time." If you have any, they're probably 15 or 30 minutes here or there.

The busyness of a working mother's schedule is one of the things that makes building and maintaining friendships hard. We just don't have time for much of a social calendar. And yet we need each other. We need the confirmation that someone understands, that someone cares about us in a special way. We need to talk about the tragedies and triumphs in our lives; to bounce ideas and options off a sympathetic ear; to complain, rejoice, laugh, or cry, knowing that someone will continue to care and support us without criticism or judgment.

We need our friends; we need the warmth of friendship in our lives. But where in that squeezed-together schedule do we fit friendship in?

According to TV commercials, all of us spend our afternoons curled up on our designer sofas in our quiet living rooms having nice, leisurely chats with our dearest friends over coffee served in our best china cups. I, for one, have trouble picturing myself in that setting. My living room is filled with the sound of TV and video games. My china teacups are stored in some remote cupboard; I use plastic cups with cartoon characters on them. As for leisurely chats—well, for me it's a big event when Karen and I can swap news over hamburgers on a hurried lunch hour!

Realistically, the leisurely living-room chats are probably out, so we're still left with the question of where we fit friendship in. I believe the answer lies in two possibilities:

First, we can make time for being with our friends by moving something else in our schedule. For example, if the garage-cleaning project can wait one more week—and who says it can't?—then maybe a friend and I can go to a movie or to the beach or the mall. If that skirt I have been planning to make isn't essential right away, that time can be spent eating pizza with friends. Working mothers know better than anyone that sometimes it is simply a matter of priorities. Unless we make friendship a priority, we cannot expect to reap its joys. If we are constantly too busy to say yes when friends ask us to do things with them, or if we never initiate any get-togethers, then we shouldn't be surprised when life starts to seem lonely.

A second option is to combine time with friends with other things we need to do. Obviously, we need to eat. Even a hurried hamburger lunch together at a fast-food stop is good for catching up on what's happening in a friend's life. If we're heading to the mall for our annual shopping-for-school-clothes trip, maybe a friend will go along.

Recently, I went to a speaking engagement in a town about an hour-and-a-half away. When I mentioned it to a friend afterwards, she said that if she had known I was going, she would have ridden up there and back with me to keep me company. I was sorry I hadn't asked her; it had never occurred to me that she would be willing to make such a big adjustment in her own busy schedule just to be with me.

*   *   *

If you want to revitalize your "support network"—that is, your circle of friends—try this, just for fun:

Jot down the names of three friends you haven't seen in a while, friends with whom you would like to touch base in some informal way. Beside each name, write a short phrase describing why it feels good to you to be with that person.

1. _____

2. _____

3. _____

Now resolve that during the next 30 days you will make contact with those individuals. Arrange to get together with them, even briefly, just to reaffirm your mutual caring and support. *Don't* let the pressure of your schedule defeat your resolution. Be creative about things the two of you can do together.

To get you started, here are some off-the-wall invitations no friend should be able to refuse:

• "My family hates Chinese food, but I love it. They're all at a baseball game, so I'm going out for sub gum duck and shrimp fried rice. Want to come along?"

• "My aerobics instructor has put together this great new routine to the entire musical score of 'Rocky.' It'll be a piece of cake. Come try it with me!"

• "My boss insists I take a two-hour computer refresher class Thursday night. I know you've been wanting to learn something about computers. Let's go!"

• "I have to find a pair of teal blue shoes to go with that

skirt you talked me into buying. I think it's your responsibility to go with me."

• "Help me clean my garage and I'll help you wash your car. Okay?"

5 ANOTHER DAY, ANOTHER DECISION

Should you let your teenage daughter go on an unchaperoned weekend camping trip with a group of friends?

Your son's school counselor has told you that your son seems to have a "personality conflict" with his history teacher. You have said you will handle it. What do you do now?

Your first-grader says she's too sick to go to school, but you have an important meeting at work today. Should you risk sending her to school anyway?

You have a chance for a job promotion, but the person who would be your new supervisor has a reputation for being supercritical and unfair. Is the promotion worth the risk?

How many times in the past year have you faced a decision—major or minor—that made you want to pull out your hair and shout in exasperation, *"Help! I just don't know what to do!"*

Working mothers repeatedly find themselves in the role of decision-maker at home and at work. Every day we face decisions we have never faced before, nor had any preparation for making.

There are the "parenting" decisions, starting with to-breast-feed-or-not-to-breast-feed and continuing up through curfew hours, dating rules, driving privileges, and college. In between are decisions about fresh versus canned baby food, bedtime, household chores, discipline, etc., etc., etc.

Then there are the work-related decisions, the ones that pertain to job possibilities, job changes, work relationships, office politics, where to go job-wise and how to get there—not to mention the day-to-day issues that arise in the course of doing our jobs.

Finally, there are the personal decisions having to do with budgeting, recreation, social life, civic or church activities, commitments to parents and other family members, and conflicting demands of work and home.

At the supermarket checkout, the cashiers always ask me if I want paper or plastic grocery sacks. I tell them, "You choose. I can't make any more decisions today."

—Lisa

Most of the time, when faced with a decision, we can't see a clear-cut "right" course of action. We agonize over pros and cons and consequences, and then after we have committed to a decision, we second-guess ourselves into sleepless nights and stressful days.

Our lives are a mosaic of decisions, both the small-but-crucial ones and the big-and-crucial ones that go with being a working mother: deciding when to punish and when to disregard, when to be firm and when to be lenient; determining the balance between your own needs and the needs of the family in any given situation;

selecting priorities; making choices from among many options.

Should I apply for that job opening with another company, and maybe jeopardize my current job situation? How much help should I give my daughter tonight with her science project that is due tomorrow? Should I buy my son an overpriced name-brand shirt just because that's what "everyone else" at his new school wears? Even though I'm not very happy with my present babysitter, they are not that easy to find; should I try to make a change? What's the best way to let my daughter know how much I disapprove of her friend Sandra?

An old cliché that has rung more and more true to me every year of my adult life is this: "There are no easy answers." Okay, so we accept that. But how do we go about finding any answers—even *hard* ones? How do we make the best possible decisions?

1. *Look at as many alternatives as you can.*

> I generally suggest to my clients that if, when they face a decision, they can see only two alternatives, it's likely that neither one is very good.
>
> —Sylvia Russell
> Mental health
> counselor

A few years ago I became thoroughly exasperated when our son repeatedly neglected to feed his cat. I had made it clear to him from the beginning that feeding the cat was to be his responsibility. There was no question that he loved his cat dearly—but he simply could not be counted on to feed him without being reminded.

I tried several different tactics to change my son's behavior. I withheld his allowance every time he forgot to feed the cat. I scolded him, pleaded with him, told him how cruel it was to make his cat go without food—you name it. Nothing worked. I was engaged in a battle of wills with a ten-year-old, and I wasn't winning.

At that point I presented my son with two alternatives: either he started being more responsible about feeding the cat, or we would give the cat away. What a silly threat! Even at his early age, my son knew that *I* was the real cat-lover in the household, and that I would never part with our furry orange family member.

When my empty threat produced zero improvement (which was no surprise), I felt I had failed miserably in my attempt to handle the situation. A relatively minor problem had become a major sore point for the whole family, causing frustration and tension all around.

"I've tried everything!" I complained to my friend Hal over lunch one day, after describing the situation. Hal, the father of two little boys, is a very firm and creative parent. I was interested in what he would say about our cat-feeding situation.

"I think I'd handle it this way," Hal said. "I'd tell my son, 'Until the cat eats, *you* don't eat.' After he misses a few meals, he'll probably remember to feed the cat."

It sounded a little too confrontational for me, but I was desperate, so I tried it.

As it turned out, coming to the table for meals served as a signal to my son, a reminder that he had a job to do. He didn't miss any meals—and neither did the cat.

In trying to deal with the situation, I had become locked into seeing only one remaining way to deal with the situation: the threat of giving the cat away—which wasn't even a realistic solution. Thankfully, my friend could see another alternative!

Try this: The next time you are facing a dilemma—whether it has to do with parenting, work, or some aspect of your personal life—try coming up with as many potential solutions as you can. Write them all down, even the ones that seem ridiculous or impractical; they may lead to other, more workable solutions. After you have completed this list, take a hard look at your ideas and eliminate the unworkable solutions—only keep the concrete solutions. Avoid options that will put you in a position of making empty threats or resolving to take actions that, for whatever reason, just are not feasible. Review the list from time to time and consider each option, then pick the best one. At least you won't end up giving away your cat!

2. *Talk to someone whose opinion you value.*

> *The way of a fool seems right to him, but a wise man listens to advice (Proverbs 12:15).*

Remember when you were pregnant and every person you met had instant advice for you about babies? Advice is a readily available commodity. You can always find people willing to tell you what they think you should do. But do you want to take their advice?

It was no accident that I happened to bring up the cat-feeding issue to Hal that day. He and I had talked many times about the trials and joys of parenting, and I had come to respect his insight and imagination. Because he and I clearly had the same goals and the same basic beliefs about rearing children, I valued his opinion.

Think about the people you know, the ones you are most likely to talk to about tough decisions you have to make. Whose opinion do you value the most? Why?

The Bible challenges us to "preserve sound judgment and discernment" (Proverbs 3:21). Nowhere is that more critical than in choosing whose advice to seek. Does he or she have your best interests at heart, or is there some self-interest involved? Can the person give you a balanced perspective, or is his/her viewpoint skewed to one side or another? For example, a coworker whose advice you seek may only be able to view your dilemma in job-related terms, not in terms of family considerations. Does the person know you well enough to fully understand the problem?

And most important: Does the person have values and beliefs similar to yours?

> *He who walks with the wise grows wise, but a companion of fools suffers harm (Proverbs 13:20).*

Decision-making can be painfully lonely. The genuine concern, the patient listening, and the caring advice of a real friend can bring a ray of light into the gloom of uncertainty. It is up to us to choose carefully whose advice we take, though.

3. *Consider postponing the decision.*

Think back to a recent decision, major or minor, that turned out to be a bad one. Maybe it was the decision to buy that olive-green blouse on a lunch-hour impulse. When you got it home you discovered that the color was not quite as flattering as you had hoped.

Or maybe it was that time you had had a month-long slump at work, a terrible stretch during which nothing seemed to go your way. One day, having had it "up to here," you called another company about a job opening they had. Nothing came of it, but a couple of weeks later, when things had improved considerably at work, you knew you really didn't want to change jobs. That was the day your supervisor called you in to say how surprised and disappointed she was that you were looking for employment elsewhere. If you had only been a little more patient, you would have found the light at the end of the tunnel.

Each of us could probably compile an embarrassingly long list of hasty decisions that proved to be unwise. Sometimes, of course, making a spur-of-the-moment decision is unavoidable. In many instances, though, by exercising an extra measure of patience and self-discipline, we can take some additional time and make a better decision.

Often we make sudden decisions when we are under some kind of emotional distress: We're fed up with conditions at work, we're frustrated because we're not getting through to our children, we're feeling depressed or angry or lonely—not good conditions for sound decision-making! When our emotions are coloring our judgment, it's a good time to consider postponing decisions.

Another cause of unwise decisions is lack of information. How many times have you heard yourself and other people say, "If only I had known"? Obviously, no one can see into the future or predict the exact results of a decision, but we can look for the information we need as the basis for our decision.

What are the facts of the situation as it is now? What would the consequences be if I chose option A, option B, or option C? What aspects of the situation do I have some control over, and which ones are outside my control? What will this decision cost me in terms of time, money, relationships—or whatever factors are involved—over the short-haul and the long-haul?

By postponing decisions when we can, we give ourselves time to get more information, to seek the advice of others, and to reflect on our options.

4. Look back over your own experience.

None of us arrives at adulthood without a rich inventory of life experience—an inventory that grows daily as we move through the stages of adult life. One of the greatest joys of my professional life has been the opportunity to advise younger people just entering their careers, to share with them some of the lessons I have learned through the years. By the same token, I have benefited greatly from the experience shared with me by people who have been in the field longer than I have. How well we make decisions must surely be related to our ability to reflect productively on our experiences.

When we face a difficult decision, we can review the catalog of our previous experience and look for something that will shed light on the problem at hand. Often, the most useful experiences are negative ones—the experiences that make us say, "I hope I never treat anyone the way that supervisor treated me" or "That's the last time I'll let myself be influenced so much by someone else's opinion."

I sure hate learning things the hard way.
—Susan

What experiences in your life most influenced your later decisions? What lessons have you learned from the most painful periods of your life? Is there some experience in the past that can help you with a decision you're facing now?

5. Prioritize your values.

Ann had a difficult decision to make. For several months she had realized she needed to make a job change. In her high-level, high-stress job, she enjoyed prestige, authority, and a very impressive salary. But during the past several months she had begun to feel more and more that her job was dominating her life. She went home at the end of the day with no energy or enthusiasm left for the family's activities or needs. As she found less and less time for her family, the level of guilt she carried around all the time increased. She was always tired and even had the beginnings of an ulcer.

Yet the job definitely had its rewards. It was challenging, and she had pulled off some very satisfying successes. She enjoyed the people she worked with and felt like a valuable member of the work team. She liked the authority she had. And she had grown very comfortably accustomed to the spending habits her salary made possible.

Still, she decided to look around and see what other opportunities might exist. After several months, she was offered a job with a small but very well-respected company. The management made it clear they felt Ann was definitely the right person to add to their staff. Unfortunately, because of the firm's small size—about one-tenth the size of her current employer—they couldn't possibly match, much less increase, her present salary. Their top offer involved a substantial pay cut. In addition, even though the position was at about the same level as her current one, because the company was so much smaller the job appeared to be a step down the career ladder instead of up.

The company badly wanted Ann's skills and experience, though, so they proposed a way to compensate for the low salary: They would give her a flexible schedule and a workweek that totaled significantly fewer hours than her present one, leaving her more time for other areas of her life. She could even leave work in time to pick up her children at school. Since they couldn't offer her more money, they were willing to give her flexibility and independence instead. Their offer began to look very tempting.

"It was a hard decision," Ann said as she looked back on it later. "First, I looked at the 'pros': the company's excellent reputation, the quality of the employees I had met, the sound company philosophy and, above all, the flexible schedule and lighter work load, which would mean less stress and pressure.

"Then," she went on, "I weighed the 'cons': the decreased responsibility due to the company's small size, the low salary, the loss of the prestige and visibility of my present job.

"Then I reexamined each 'pro' and 'con.' I realized that the high level of responsibility at my present job was largely the cause of the stress and pressure, so having less responsibility really wasn't a minus at all— except in terms of my own ego. The same was true of the idea that I was taking a step backward. I had to ask myself, 'So what? Backward in whose book?' That was just my ego talking, too. So the only 'con' left was the salary. Every rule of the job game says you make job changes to get higher salaries, not lower ones. Everyone thought I was crazy even to consider it.

"So I ended up weighing the factors all again. The pluses were: a schedule that allowed more time for my family, a less stressful work environment—which meant more energy for other things—and, in general, a more balanced life. The only minus left was the salary.

"When I looked at it that way, it became obvious that I was trying to measure the value of my own and my family's well-being against a dollar amount. I was actually considering making a decision that would give money more importance than meeting their needs and my needs.

" 'No way,' I finally told myself. I called and accepted the job. It's been over a year, and I haven't regretted it for a second. Sure, I miss the extra money, but we've all adjusted. I'm much better off mentally, physically, and emotionally, and I think my family is benefiting, too. As a bonus, I'm even saving money on after-school care for the kids!

"To be honest, I'm embarrassed to think that I almost put money ahead of people's needs—mine and my family's. That's scary. I sure have learned something about setting priorities."

> *But godliness with contentment is great gain.*
> *For we brought nothing into the world, and we*
> *can take nothing out of it. But if we have*
> *food and clothing, we will be content with*
> *that. People who want to get rich fall into*
> *temptation and a trap and into many foolish*
> *and harmful desires... (1 Timothy 6:6).*

Not everyone has the options Ann had in choosing her job change. When we look at our financial needs, we may feel that, regardless of what priorities we set, we have no choices at all about our work situation. That's seldom the case. While we may not have a choice about whether to work outside the home or not, we have a wide range of other choices. The choice of how we view our work and what role it has in our lives is always ours. We can grit our teeth and grimly accept going to work every day, or we can look for the value of what we do and the good in the people with whom we work. We can take pride in doing our work well, or we can invest just enough effort to do a passable job.

Sometimes we fall victim to a kind of fatalistic laziness that says, "I'm stuck in this job. I'll never get out," when in reality we could be looking for something else. Unless our financial situation is truly critical, isn't it better to make a few dollars less a year in a job we enjoy than to spend 40 hours a week in a job we hate? Life's just too short for that.

It frustrates me to hear people I know groan about the long hours they have to work, when I know that they are individuals who choose to invest all their energy in their jobs instead of maintaining balance between work and other areas of their lives. Their families feel abandoned, their church and civic responsibilities are neglected, and they wear themselves out physically and mentally. Yet they see themselves as victims of the demands of their jobs rather than as victims of their own choices. Most of these people do make a lot of money—but it's sad to see what it's costing them.

The experience surrounding her job change gave Ann a chance to think about her own values. In considering her decision, she had to prioritize the many factors involved: job prestige, finances, family commitments, ego and "strokes," balance between work and other demands, career goals and needs. Not a simple decision. The big ones seldom are.

What is important to you? When you face a major decision, what is the bottom line? Is it money? Family needs? Career progress? Self-esteem? Your overall well-being, however you define it?

> Life is difficult enough without doing things to make it more so.
>
> —Pat

We make life more difficult than it has to be if we let ourselves continually make decisions in a vacuum; that is, without a clear sense of priorities and values. It's like reinventing the wheel *and* the automobile every time we want to go for a drive.

Unless we understand the fundamental values we want to teach our children, we have to start from scratch every time we need to discipline them or make a decision about what they will be allowed to do. Unless we define for ourselves the role of work in our lives, every major job-related decision will be a strain. Unless we commit to a clear set of principles to guide our daily living, our days will be filled with uncertainty and confusion. That's a hard way to live.

In the remaining chapters, we will look at some values and priorities that have stood the test of time, so that we won't have to make our decisions in a vacuum. As Pat says, life is difficult enough!

6 THE RELATIVE IMPORTANCE OF SOCKS

Have you ever had a fantasy in which you left work one day and didn't go back—just walked off the job and let the chips fall? No resignation, no two weeks notice, no wrapping up all the loose ends of things you were working on. Just walking out the door for good.

Maybe I shouldn't admit it, but I have. (Note: I never really did it, though.) I think that, among other things, it's a way of trying to reaffirm my own sense that what I do at work is important. If suddenly I'm not there to make my daily contribution to the organization, then theoretically the value of what I do will be more evident to others. "They'll appreciate me when I'm gone" is the underlying reasoning, childish as it might sound.

What if you "walked off the job" at home? Would anyone notice? Do you ever feel like you could just vanish and no one would even know it until the clean socks ran out or the peanut butter jar was empty?

Sometimes it is very hard to maintain a sense that what we do at home or on the job matters to anyone. We spend our hours at work and our hours at home doing, doing, doing, and no one says, "Gee, thanks for preparing that report" or "Wow, Mom, I sure appreciate your taking me to soccer practice." Some days I want to wear a sign that says, *"Hey, does anybody care that I'm doing all this?"*

> There was a time in my life, when my children were small, that I honestly felt I wasn't good for anything except wiping noses and bottoms.
>
> —Pat

When we feel that the things in which we invest our time and effort don't matter, our self-esteem takes a beating. We may begin to doubt, as Pat did, our own ability to do anything worthwhile. We may begin to care less and less about the quality of what we do because we wonder if it makes any difference. Our daily tasks may start to seem like meaningless rituals that we do over and over again without even thinking about them.

Washing the same dinner plate the umpteenth night in a row. Laundering the same socks and underwear week after week. Answering the phone at work the same way 20 times a day and filling out the same paperwork. We can get so bogged down in *tasks* that we begin to see life as one long "to do" list. Each day is simply a sequence of tasks we have to do, only to go to bed, get up, and repeat them the next day.

What we do *is* important. No, washing plates and socks won't change the world. Phone calls and paperwork are not going to revolutionize civilization. But the total product of what we do—in the course of a day, or a week, or a year or a lifetime—is important. When we shift our focus from the tasks themselves to the bigger picture, we can see that *what we do is important because it represents an investment of God-given resources.*

As we discussed in chapter 1, God has an investment in us. Our very being is from Him. He gave us life; He created the world in which we live. Each day He gives us time, talent, mental and physical ability, energy, spiritual strength, material possessions—all the resources that enable us to accomplish the things we do, whether it's finishing a task at work or keeping our households afloat. Recognizing that everything we do is an expenditure of His investment in us gives us a twofold perspective: 1) the responsibility of spending our—His—resources wisely, and 2) the assurance that He cares about what we do because the capacity to do it comes from Him. Our lives are not meaningless; therefore, the things we do aren't either.

What we do is *important because God has given us the task of preparing a new generation for life.*

Sometimes the awesome responsibility of being a parent scares me. When I realize that my son's view of life and the course of his future will depend largely on me, it is terrifying. The opinions I express, the way I treat people and the things I say about them, the habits I have, the rules I set for my household—virtually everything I do or say—influences him. That fact alone makes all those things important. I find myself thinking, "I'm not good enough to be worthy of that incredible responsibility!"

Then I remember that I don't have to rely on my own wisdom, knowledge, or insight to carry out the job of being a parent. God is willing and ready to help. If I try to live by His guidelines and teach my son to follow them, then I have fulfilled my important role as a mother the best I can.

> *Train a child in the way he should go, and when he is old he will not turn from it*
> *(Proverbs 22:6).*

What we do is important because we are uniquely equipped to do it.

Something that always disturbs me is hearing someone say, "I'm just a _____." If they work for a big company, they might say, "I'm just a clerk" or "I'm just a mail sorter." Some women say, "I'm just a housewife." They clearly express the view that what they do is not important, or at least is not as important as what someone else does.

Yet God created human beings and His world in such a way that every person's contribution is unique and valuable. The apostle Paul described this scheme of things vividly in his first letter to the Corinthians, comparing people to parts of the human body:

> Now the body is not made up of one part but of many.... If the whole body were an eye, where would the sense of hearing be? If the whole body were an ear, where would the sense of smell be? But in fact God has arranged the parts of the body, every one of them, just as he wanted them to be.... As it is, there are many parts, but one body (1 Corinthians 12:14,17-19).

Think about the people you know. What special abilities, personality traits, skills, or experience do they contribute to the whole, whether the whole is your home, your place of work, your church, or simply your circle of friends?

> What is man that you are mindful of him, the son of man that you care for him? You made him a little lower than the heavenly beings and crowned him with glory and honor. You made him ruler over the works of your hands; you put everything under his feet (Psalm 8:4-6).

You are important. Your place in God's scheme of things is important, and what you do is important. Now, knowing that, let's look at prioritizing the things we do, so that we concentrate our time and energy on the most important of those things.

How Do I Get There from Here?

My jobs over the years have often involved developing and writing plans—marketing plans, program plans, plans for special events, etc. It didn't take me long to find out that the first step in writing any kind of plan is setting goals. We have to choose our destination before we leave on the trip, whether the "trip" is our family's vacation or selling a new product for the company. Once the goals (the "destination") of the plan have been identified, then the steps that will take us from here to there can be carried out.

How about you? What's your destination? What life goals do you have for yourself?

Here's a sampling of some goals that a working mother might have. Underline the ones that you share. Then in the space provided jot down some additional ones of your own.

Goals

- *To have my children be happy, healthy, well-adjusted human beings.*

- *To cultivate trust, loyalty, and mutual support in my marriage, with my children, and in my other important relationships.*

- *To equip my children for life by passing on to them the values I cherish and to help them avoid the mistakes I have made.*

- *To develop spiritual strength and maturity.*

- *To have a job that is satisfying and meaningful to me, and to be rewarded in my career as my skill and knowledge increase.*

- *To contribute to the financial well-being of my family and enable them to have the things they need and want.*

- *To help provide both emotional and material security for my family.*

- *To make a contribution to this world and leave it a better place than I found it.*

- *To enjoy life.*

- *To develop and cultivate deep friendships.*

- *To be known as a person who cares about others.*

- *To realize my own potential and help my loved ones realize theirs.*

- *Additional goals:*

  _____

  _____

  _____

  _____

  _____

  _____

Now that we have identified our major goals, let's look at how the things we do either move us toward those goals or hinder our progress.

I have a theory. You won't find it in your old geometry workbook or in any philosophy text (because now, even as you are reading this, it is being introduced to the world for the first time). Still, I think there's something to it. I call it the "Theory of Harmonious Congruence of Temporal Realities Versus Metaphysical Precepts Extrapolated into Cognitive Associations," or "How to Avoid Wasting Time and Effort on Things that Aren't Important."

Now, if this theory had appeared in your high school geometry book, it would have looked like this:

$$T = 1/M$$

T stands for time; M stands for importance. Stated in plain English, the theory is that the amount of time we spend doing, thinking, and/or worrying about a given task is often inversely proportional to the importance of the task.

In my life, this theory applies especially well to two things: cooking and having company.

I don't cook much. It's not that I can't; I'm really not a bad cook, but it's not a priority for me. I get home from work late in the day, tired, wanting to sit for a minute and unwind, and the idea of planning and executing a major dinner isn't very appealing. As a result, my family eats a lot of fast food, canned food, and frozen food. (I do thaw it out first.)

The problem isn't that we eat hamburgers and Spaghetti-O's. The problem is that because of the way we eat, I spend a lot of time worrying about whether my family is getting proper nutrition, whether I'm a poor mother because I don't give them home-cooked meals, whether I'm selfish not to make the effort to cook them dinner, etc. All that guilt and worrying is incredibly unproductive.

The theory holds true. The issue of whether I cook or don't cook isn't important at all. Nowhere in my personal list of life goals is there anything that even remotely suggests that cooking is or should be one of my priorities. The amount of time I spend thinking and/or worrying about it is all out of proportion to the importance of cooking in my life. See how the theory works?

I think the secret is to lower your expectations.
                                              —Joanne

I'm still struggling with the cooking business, but when it comes to having company, I think I have myself under control. In days gone by, if someone called and said, "I'm stopping by tonight," I would launch myself into a flurry of cleaning: picking up every item not in its proper place; dusting every surface, vacuuming, scrubbing the kitchen and bathroom counters, the works. By the time the company arrived, the house looked great, but I was exhausted. I barely had time before the doorbell rang to put on a clean blouse, and I was not in any state to be a gracious—or enthusiastic—hostess.

After more than enough years of the no-one-can-see-my-house-unless-it's-cleaned-up approach, I decided that enjoying my guests was more important than cleaning. It occurred to me that I was doing my friends a disservice to assume that they would think less of me if there was an empty pop bottle on the dining room table or a three-day-old newspaper on the sofa. One of my goals is to cultivate and maintain satisfying friendships; rushing around in frantic, last-minute cleaning binges was not going to help me meet that goal. In terms of the theory $T = 1/M$, I was spending too much time and energy on the cleaning and not enough on the friendships.

Enough of my true confessions. Now let's talk about you. Go back to the goals you listed earlier. By each one, write down some specific tasks you can do to help yourself meet that goal.

Now, in another space write down some of the tasks or emotions that take up your time and/or energy but don't move you toward any of your goals. This may take some serious soul-searching, but it will be worth it. After you have identified some of those things, consider how to work them out of your life or change your handling of them so they don't consume a disproportionate amount of your personal resources.

Just to give yourself a manageable task for the time being, in the space below write down *one thing* you want to change this week about the way you spend your time and energy. Focus on some change that will help you move closer to one of your major goals, your destination, something that will enable you to spend more of your time on what is *important* to you!

_____

_____

He Knew Where He Was Going

Jesus had a powerful sense of His destination. Everything He did was geared to accomplishing what He had set out to do. In fact, He compared His goal in life to food. Carrying out His mission on earth was as essential to Him as eating. His goal was simply to do the work God had sent Him to do, and as His life neared its end, He said to God in a prayer, "I have brought you glory on earth by completing the work you gave me to do" (John 17:4).

Think about the unique gifts God has given you, the importance His love and care have built into everything you do. What a relief from constantly wondering, "Does any of this matter? Is it really important?" When we choose to acknowledge God as our Creator and recognize His sovereignty in our lives, then our work—whatever our day-to-day efforts might be—becomes His work. And *that's* important.

7 FREE AT LAST, OR LAST TO BE FREE?

The Freedom Dream

Roberta feels trapped.

When she first took this job four years ago, she had a whole smorgasbord of challenges ahead of her: hiring new staff, designing new procedures, reviewing policies, and making recommendations. She had a real sense of moving forward as each new idea began to take shape.

Now, she feels imprisoned by the very changes that challenged her before. Her supervisors don't seem to want any more changes. Now that the procedures are in place, everyone seems locked into the status quo. Each week she goes to the same meetings, sees the same people, moves the same forms from the "in" box to the "out" box. She feels like a hamster in a cage, running around and around in her little metal wheel, locked into the same circular path day after day.

Life at home, unfortunately, seems about the same. Dinner is always rushed and hectic; even when she and Jim and the kids eat out, it's at the same fast-food places because that's all the kids will eat. She and Jim haven't gone to a movie in ages because there never seems to be a free night between Randy's baseball games and Susan's track meets and her mother-in-law's family dinners every weekend. Her evenings and weekends seem to be eaten away by little necessities—picking up around the house, stopping at the store, laundry, dental appointments, juggling bills, the kids' commitments.

Roberta finds herself daydreaming about what it would be like to be free, just for a short time—no locked-in schedule, no demands, no rules about who or what or where she needs to be.

Is my life going to be like this forever? she wonders. *Will I ever have any real freedom? Or did I unknowingly trade it away when I became a working mother? Do I have to wait until I'm retired and the kids are grown? I don't think I can last that long.*

Does Roberta's daydream strike home? All of us can probably identify in one way or another with her sense of constantly straining against things that lock her in or tie her down.

Would it surprise you to know that what God wants for us is to be free?

> *It is for freedom that Christ has set us free.*
> *Stand firm, then, and do not let yourselves be*
> *burdened again by a yoke of slavery*
> *(Galatians 5:1).*

Working mothers' lives are filled with potential "enslavers"—not necessarily people, but rather ideas, feelings, circumstances, and behavior patterns that make them feel limited or closed in.

Although the writer of the verse above was referring to the slavery of legalistic religious thinking, his word of caution pertains just as aptly to other potential "enslavers" in our lives. It is interesting that he warns us not to *let* ourselves be enslaved. His choice of words suggests that, to a great extent, we can make choices that either maintain or compromise our personal freedom. We can choose to let circumstances, people, expectations, invalid beliefs, false images and other forces confine us unnecessarily, or we can choose to pursue the freedom God wants us to have: freedom to live the "abundant life" He promised us and freedom to be the whole, unique persons He created us to be.

In this and the next two chapters, we will examine some of the specific elements in our lives that erode our sense of freedom, and explore ways to keep them from enslaving us. First, though, let's look at some basic steps in cultivating and maintaining a sense of freedom.

1. Identify the things that make you feel trapped.

We have little hope of changing the things that make us feel enslaved if we cannot determine what they are. Maybe it is some circumstance of our daily lives, like our tight, predictable schedules or our endless chauffeuring. Is it facing the same routine tasks at home and at work day after day? Is it the lack of time to do things for ourselves, just for fun? Is it shuttling back and forth between work, school, home, and the supermarket with no change of scene?

Or perhaps it's something less easily defined. Is it the demands we place on ourselves to be all things to all people? Is it a set of unrealistic expectations about who and what we need to be? Is it a sense that if we are not perfect all the time—if we lose our temper or say "no" without a perfectly logical reason—then we are dismal failures? Is it trying to squeeze ourselves into someone else's box of "shoulds"?

It is very easy to misplace the blame for our feelings of being tied down. Often we want to lay the blame on our spouses, our children, our in-laws, or our bosses. In reality it may be circumstances, expectations, routines, or attitudes—and not people at all—that make us feel hemmed in. Fortunately, these things are usually much easier to change than people. If we can identify the sources of our feelings of nonfreedom, we can take steps toward change.

2. Develop and maintain friendships.

Loneliness is often a by-product of feeling trapped. As we grow to feel imprisoned by the routines and demands of our daily lives, we feel cut off from other people. So much effort goes into just staying on course with our daily commitments that we don't make time to maintain friendship and communication—the very things we need for support. As a result, at a time when we need the company and understanding of other people the most, we have the least of it.

When my husband was in law school, our situation was very confining. He went to school full-time and was either in class or studying day and night, seven days a week. I worked full-time while trying to be both mother and father to our preschool-age son. The saving grace of that time in our lives was the friendship of other students and their spouses. Among the people we knew and associated with, everyone's life was defined by the same tight budgets, long hours of studying, job pressures, parenting responsibilities, and limited social lives. When things felt like too much to handle, there was always someone who understood perfectly, someone who could honestly say, "I know exactly how you feel." Looking back, we cherish those friendships, and know those years would have been much more difficult without these special people.

In chapter 5 we discussed the many reasons working mothers need each other. By supporting and encouraging one another, we prevent the loneliness and isolation that can make our lives feel unnecessarily confining.

3. Let others help.

When my son was small, my friend Barb used to take care of him for me occasionally so that I could have some time on my own. Her own children were in high school, and she enjoyed having a toddler to entertain now and then. I told her one day that I wished she still had a toddler herself so that I could repay her for her help.

"When my kids were little," she said, "a woman in my neighborhood named Maggie took care of them for me sometimes, just so I could get out of the house and do whatever I wanted or needed to do. She was several years older than I was, and her children were grown. She never let me pay her for babysitting. When I said, 'How can I repay you?' she said, 'Just do the same for someone else sometime.'

"So that's what I'm doing. Consider it a gift from Maggie."

Working mothers, on the whole, are an independent bunch. We are so used to juggling tasks, being responsible, and keeping ourselves and other people on schedule that we grow unaccustomed to letting someone help us. The fact is, asking for help isn't a crime. Neither is accepting it when it's offered.

For some reason, it took me a long time to learn that it's okay to let my friends help me.
—Kathy

I'm always delighted when another mother calls me and says, "I'm in a jam at work; can you pick up the kids at baseball practice?" or "My husband and I really want to get away for the weekend. Can my son stay with you?" First of all, I feel flattered that she feels comfortable calling me. It tells me she considers me a good enough friend to be willing to help. Second, when I have had a chance to help someone else out, I feel more free to call her when I'm in a bind myself.

Being a working mother is tough enough without insisting on doing it all single-handedly. Our spouses, our friends, our parents, even our kids, can be called on to help now and then. And maybe—just maybe—they will be pleased to be asked!

4. *Check your focus.*

Not being much of a photographer, I was having a frustrating time trying to shoot pictures of my son's baseball game through the wire-mesh fence surrounding the playing field. When I looked through the viewfinder, all I saw was gray metal wire with a green-shirted blur in the background. As I experimented with the adjustable focus, though, I found that if I focused *past* the fence, on my son, the fence faded into an almost unnoticeable blur and my little first baseman became clear. What had seemed like a major obstacle became a minor distraction.

I think the "fences" that seem to limit our freedom can be dealt with in much the same way. If we focus on the limitations and demands that our responsibilities place on us, we can't expect to experience a sense of freedom. But if we shift our focus to the things within and outside us that are not subject to those limitations, the barriers recede.

Children are amazing and wonderful creatures. They grow and unfold each day, giving us ever-new glimpses of the adults they will become. When we let ourselves focus too much on the demands and constraints of parent-hood—and you and I know they do exist—we run the risk of missing out on that miraculous day-to-day revelation.

The same is true of ourselves. We see what we are, but God sees what we can be. When we focus exclusively on our limitations instead of our unique gifts, we miss out on the growth and challenge He has in store for us. When we focus on what we cannot do because we haven't enough time or money or energy or talent, we become blind to the vast potential of what we *can* do. Unlike ours, God's vision for us has no limits!

> *For you created my inmost being; you knit me*
> *together in my mother's womb. I praise you*
> *because I am fearfully and wonderfully made;*
> *your works are wonderful... (Psalm 139:13,14).*

5. Go the distance.

Imagine yourself standing in the middle of a cornfield in summer. (If you grew up in the Midwest, this is an easy one. If you grew up in Newark, it may take a little more effort.) All you can see around you is corn. The cornstalks are taller than you are, so you can't see over them. If you kneel down and look along the stalks just above the soil, all you see are rows and rows of the same, stretching into what seems like infinity. A foot above the ground the stalks and ears and husks are so thick you can't see more than a few feet in any direction. There are no landmarks, no variations, so you have no way to get your bearings or find a way out. You feel trapped.

Now imagine that you are in an airplane, flying over that same cornfield. It doesn't look anything like it did from the ground. Now it's just a square, green-striped patch on a quilt of the countryside. It really isn't very big. On one side there's a gravel road and you can see a small dust cloud being stirred up by a pickup truck. On another side there's a two-lane highway. The third side is bounded by woods and the fourth by an open field where a few cows are grazing.

From your new vantage point several thousand feet in the air, it is hard to imagine how you could have felt so trapped in that little square of cornfield. Putting some distance between yourself and the corn makes a lot of difference.

A working mother's life can seem like that cornfield. There we are, right in the thickest part of it, hemmed in by seemingly endless rows of things to do. We look ahead, we look behind us, we look around us, and all we see are tasks to do, responsibilities to fulfill, and needs to meet. I believe that from time to time we need to find a way to look at our lives from a distance so we can see what the boundaries really are and regain an accurate perspective. Only when we take time to let our day-to-day concerns and pressures dissipate can we focus on the bigger picture. By stepping back and becoming observers of our own lives, we can better see the patterns, the pitfalls, and the progress we are making toward our goals.

Somehow as the pace of life has increased to fever pitch, we have almost come to regard getting away and taking time for reflection as self-indulgent or a luxury. It isn't. It's essential. The Bible tells us that even Jesus withdrew from the crowds around Him and spent time in contemplation and solitude.

What would it take to give you that distance from which to observe your own life? A weekend getaway? A real go-somewhere-and-sit-by-the-lake vacation? An evening all to yourself when the family is away and the house is quiet? A trip to a park or a scenic spot, away from the hustle and bustle? An extra hour set aside early in the morning each day for a week?

Give it some thought. Sometimes it takes distance to give us a close-up view of our own lives. Find a way to give yourself that distance.

When you're in the middle of the cornfield, all you can see is the corn.

—Elsa

---

6. *Recharge.*

In watching those TV commercials that show how one brand of batteries lasts longer than another, do you always identify with the toy that runs down first? Then maybe you need to recharge!

Recharging is a way of asserting the freedom to take care of our own needs. It is a way of recognizing that we cannot attend to the needs of other people if we let ourselves run out of emotional and physical energy.

Some people find that exercise helps them recharge; others feel renewed by the arts: a concert, an exhibit, a play. People who volunteer for community or church activities often find that those activities refresh and restore their spirits. What works for you? Or has your schedule become so locked up by external demands that you have neglected the needs within yourself? If you don't have periodic chances for "recharging" built into your schedule, resolve to do it now!

Freedom Within, Freedom Without

The suggestions listed above can help us maintain a sense of freedom in our outward lives. But what about inner freedom?

When God created us in His image—to be reflections of Him—inner freedom was included in the package. The Book of Genesis tells us that after He created human beings, He said, "...let them rule over the fish of the sea and the birds of the air, over the livestock, over all the earth..." (1:26). Does that sound as though He wants us to let our spirits be enslaved by the pressures and constraints of daily life?

Job demands, home and family commitments, and limitations on time, talent, and money are all very real. We have to live within the boundaries of our lives. But we don't have to give up our freedom to do so.

Freedom to realize our unique potential, freedom to see what is best in other people, freedom to make a contribution to our world, to make a difference in someone else's life, to savor the sight of a rainbow—that's the freedom God has given us. That freedom isn't limited by tight budgets, overcrowded schedules, flagging energy, or tedious routines. The only limits on that freedom are the ones we impose on ourselves and the ones we let be imposed by other forces.

Inherent in the freedom God gives us is the freedom to make choices. First and foremost, we can choose to do the things He wants us to do—to live by the guidelines He established for His world—or we can choose not to. We can choose to follow the example of Jesus, whom God sent to show us how to live, or we can wander through life, directionless and purposeless, desperately looking for meaning in work or money or relationships. When we turn our backs on God, we lose the freedom He meant for us to have. We open ourselves up to enslavement by destructive forces like immorality, selfishness, envy, greed, and all the things that make for an unhappy, unsatisfying life.

> *Then choose for yourselves this day whom you will serve.... But as for me and my household, we will serve the Lord.*
>
> —*The prophet Joshua*
> *(Joshua 24:15)*

Yes, the many demands on our time, energy, and spirit can make us feel trapped. We may have to work for a sense of freedom in our outward, day-to-day lives. But freedom in our inner worlds is a gift from God, earmarked for us long before we were ever born. To receive it, we have only to choose to do so.

Finding the Freedom Factor: An Exercise

1. On the whole, I would describe the sense of freedom in my life as:

   ( ) nonexistent   ( ) occasional
   ( ) most of the time ( ) all the time*

   *If you checked this choice, go directly to chapter 10.

2. I feel the *least* free when _____

   _____.

3. I think I would feel more free if I could _____

   _____.

4. Realistically, here are three changes I can make that I think would give me a greater sense of freedom:

   a. _____

   b. _____

   c. _____

5. I'm going to start making those changes on (date)

   _____.

6. Knowing that God wants me to be free makes me feel

   _____.

7. As I have read this chapter and thought about freedom in my life, the most important thing I have discovered is _____.

   _____

8. I think this discovery (in #7) will be helpful to me the next time I _____.

8 THE RISKS OF ROUTINE

It has always amazed me to see how much small children enjoy having the same story read to them over and over. They never seem to tire of hearing the same events told again and again. Adults, on the other hand, aren't nearly so crazy about repetition. Many years ago when I was babysitting one afternoon, I was reading a story for the umpteenth time and fell asleep right in the middle of it. Guess I had heard it enough!

A lot of the things we do every day produce a feeling much like having the same story read to us over and over. We drive the same routes to work, to school, to the grocery store, to the dry cleaners, and home again. We get up at the same time every morning and dress in the same style. We say the same things to our children day after day. ("Did you brush your teeth?" "Put the milk away." "Be home by 11.") We even exchange the same remarks with our coworkers every workday. ("Have a good evening." "I can't believe this rain." "Love your outfit." "This coffee is terrible.")

> Once, just once, I'd like to show up at work wearing a chartreuse suit and an orange tie.
>
> —Jim

We repeat the same tasks day after day, too. Standing at my kitchen sink one night, I actually considered the idea that it was a waste of time to wash dishes because we would just dirty them again anyway. The whole cycle of washing dishes, putting them away, taking them out, putting food on them, and washing them again suddenly just seemed infinitely futile. Fortunately, I snapped out of it before I tried serving dinner on unwashed plates.

Not just our day-to-day actions but our thinking can fall into routine patterns, too. For some reason, it seems to be easier to let our minds drift into thinking about problems, worries, and other "negatives" in our lives than to focus on the upbeat and the positive. When the alarm goes off in the morning we think, "Another day. What a drag." Driving to work, we groan over facing a difficult boss one more day or having to finish a troublesome assignment. Driving home, we mentally list all the demands that face us that evening, or fume over some unpleasant incident at work. Before we fall asleep, we haul out the "worry sack" and mull over our problems, ending our day on an unhappy note.

I visited a forest in Colorado once where there was an old logging road used by trucks coming in to load the cut timber. Over the years, the tires of heavily-loaded trucks had worn two deep parallel grooves in the road, and each new truck using it had to keep its tires in the same ruts or the road would be too difficult to travel. So naturally, the ruts grew deeper with each passing truck.

Does this pattern ring a bell?

It is easy to see how the "ruts" in our day-to-day lives come into being. We do the same things day after day, and the more habitual they become, the more difficult it becomes to break out of them. Before we know it, we may feel trapped, locked unnecessarily into patterns of acting and thinking that limit our ability to enjoy life.

I think if I put myself on autopilot for one day,
no one—including me—would even notice.
—Kelly

I don't think God meant for our lives to be boring or
confining or for us to be trapped by routines and patterns. He gave us the ability to be creative and to make
decisions for ourselves. He gave us eyes to see, ears to
hear, and senses to experience His creation in its infinite
variety. He gave us emotions that allow us to laugh and
cry and feel what it means to be human.

There's real danger in letting ourselves become so
locked in by routines or patterns—whether of thinking
or of doing—that we fail to notice and enjoy the good
things around us. The challenge of being human is a
challenge to keep growing, keep changing, keep learning. When we sit back and let that challenge pass us by, we
give up some of our freedom to experience the rich and
satisfying life God wants us to have.

Certainly we don't need or want to break out of all our
routines. In my family when we talk on the phone, we
always end the conversation with "I love you." I hope I
never break out of that pattern! Work has its inescapable
patterns, too, and often following established routines is
simply part of the job. The key, whether at work or in
other areas of our lives, is to distinguish between the
routines and patterns that are useful, necessary, and/or
satisfying, and the ones that are confining, boring, or
even destructive. The next step, then, is to decide what
can be changed and make the effort to change it.

One of the most unproductive patterns I ever fell into
was the habit of leaving the office and, while driving
home, reviewing all the day's problems—tense relationships, seemingly impossible assignments, conflicts,

everything negative. It was an especially difficult time at work, and over a period of several weeks, I grew tightly locked into that habit. The realization that I needed to break out of that particular pattern came very suddenly; it literally crashed in on me, in fact. In the space of one month, I had two minor car accidents, both of them directly caused by my being too preoccupied with work problems to pay attention to the cars in front of me!

Our lives do consist largely of routines, which are neither good nor bad in themselves; they're just there. Whether routines turn into ruts depends less on the routines themselves than on what we do with them.

It's time for another exercise. Think about the routines in your own life. In the space below jot down five routines or patterns that are meaningful or pleasant for you. They can be little things like a quiet cup of coffee before work, or bigger things like vacationing in the same place or celebrating birthdays in the same way each year. (If you can't think of any existing ones, how about creating some new ones?)

1. _____

2. _____

3. _____

4. _____

5. _____

Now, what about the routines you don't like—the ones that make you feel trapped or just plain bored or irritated? They might be things like: getting up at the same time every morning and going through the same motions as you get ready for work; doing laundry every Monday night or every Saturday morning, white clothes first, then colors, then darks; bringing a ham sandwich and a diet Coke to work every single day for lunch, and eating it in the same lunchroom with the same people. Write down some of those less-than-pleasant routines here:

1. _____
2. _____
3. _____
4. _____
5. _____

It's time to be creative. How can you change these patterns to give yourself the feeling of breaking out of a rut? There are very few areas of our lives in which we don't have choices and can't make changes, however small. Beside each item listed above, jot down a note about how you can change it.

Now that we have looked at some specific routines, let's talk about general ways to keep routine as a whole from bogging us down and taking the fun out of daily living.

1. *Start each day with a sense of anticipation.*

Try this short quiz: Check the reaction below that sounds most like you when it's time to get up and go to work.

( ) Reaction #1: *"Blech. Another day at the zoo."*

( ) Reaction #2: *"I think I feel a cold coming on. Maybe if I gargle with Comet I'll be convincing when I call in sick."*

( ) Reaction #3: *"I guess it wouldn't hurt to hit the snooze alarm just one more time."*

( ) Reaction #4: *"This is all just a bad dream. I'm actually retired and living in Bermuda."*

( ) Reaction #5: *"Is that a cloud I see out the window? Must be a terrible (rain, snow, hail—choose one) storm coming. I'm sure the road to the office will be impassable and it's just a matter of time until the police request that everyone stay at home. It's my civic duty."*

( ) Reaction #6: *"Oh. It's time to get up and go to work. Gee."*

( ) Reaction #7: *"Oh, wow, another workday! Gosh, I'd better get up! I don't want to waste a single minute!"* *

(*If you checked this answer, you are in for a long and happy working life and will probably be president of your own Fortune 500 company someday. Go directly to chapter 9.)

Our tendency to fall into "thinking routines" is very evident in our reaction to the sound of the alarm or whatever tells us it's time to get up and go to work. As you think about it now, isn't it true that you generally greet each day with the same thought patterns?

A day that begins under a cloud of black thoughts is automatically off to a bad start. What if we were to think instead about what the day might have in store—a memorable moment with one of our children, a glimpse of spring after a long winter, a chance for a new friendship at work, or an opportunity for kindness? Even if we know the day holds problems or tensions, we can still greet it in a spirit of hope and optimism.

The Book of Psalms, a collection of ancient songs and prayers, captures this eager anticipation of each day. The psalms reflect their writers' overwhelming sense of expectation; we can almost picture him eagerly waiting to see what God will do that day. Even when his days were filled with trouble, the psalmist faced them with the same confidence that God was at work and present in his life.

God is at work today just as He was in the psalmist's time. We can start each day with the same confidence of being in God's care and the same sense of expectancy as we wait to see what He has in store for us. Wouldn't that start a day off better than "You-mean-I-have-to-get-up-and-go-to-work-again?"

If you want to make some changes in the thinking patterns that start your days, try this: Copy one or more of the verses below (they are all from the psalms) onto a card and tape it up someplace where you will see it first thing each morning. Keep it there for a week. At the end of the week, take some time to reflect on how it felt to begin each day with that thought. Then choose a different verse to post for the following week. Here are some possible verses from which to choose:

Morning by morning, O Lord, you hear my voice; morning by morning I lay my requests before you and wait in expectation (5:3).

Shout for joy to the Lord, all the earth. Serve the Lord with gladness; come before him with joyful songs (100:1,2).

I call on you, O God, for you will answer me; give ear to me and hear my prayer (17:6).

Surely God is my help; the Lord is the one who sustains me (54:4).

Sing to the Lord a new song, for he has done marvelous things (98:1).

The Lord reigns, let the earth be glad (97:1).

Come and see what God has done, how awesome his works in man's behalf! (66:5).

2. *Enjoy the pleasant routines in your life.*

> In my family we have a routine about giving compliments. Whenever I compliment one of the kids on something—if I say, for example, "I like your dress"—I always add, "and I like you, too."
>
> —Pat

Look again at the routines you listed above as being positive and satisfying for you. Think about what makes them enjoyable. Resolve not to let them turn into ruts!

My friend Jackie spends literally hours each week in the car, driving her high-school-age daughter to and from her many activities in various parts of the city. "Doesn't that get awfully tiresome?" I asked her once.

"Not at all!" she said. "In fact, I look forward to it. It's the only time I have Vicki all to myself, when she and I can talk without interruptions. I get to hear what she thinks about things, what's going on at school and with her friends. I know that time together is one of the things I'll miss most when she leaves for college."

Positive routines can be important threads in the fabric of family life. Let's cultivate and cherish them!

3. *Try a fresh approach.*

"Brainstorming" is a popular technique in the corporate world today. Usually it involves getting members of a department or work group together, presenting them with a specific problem or goal, and letting them come up with as many creative solutions or approaches as possible without worrying about details like how much it costs, whether it's against the rules, who is going to carry it out, etc. All ideas receive equal consideration, regardless of how outlandish or how mundane; criticism of other people's ideas or negative remarks like "Yes, but..." are not allowed.

When it comes to the routines in our lives that are tedious or frustrating or unproductive, maybe we can learn something from the brainstorming technique. What if you simply looked at the purpose of the routine—what you need to accomplish—and tried out some new ways of accomplishing it?

Example: Kevin, age 10, hates to shop. The annual routine of taking him shopping for school clothes at the end of each summer always ends up being a test of his mother's patience and self-control. Kevin simply doesn't like browsing through racks and racks of clothes, and because he dislikes shopping to begin with, none of the clothes appeal to him. His demeanor throughout the trip is discreetly sulky; he would much rather be at home playing video games.

As a result, Teresa, his mother, feels as though she is begging him to let her spend hard-earned money on clothes he neither wants nor likes, and may or may not wear. She briefly considers letting him wear four-inches-too-short pants and catsup-stained shirts throughout the fifth grade, but can't bring herself to do it. Both of them end up feeling frustrated and resentful. Not a happy outcome.

Suppose Teresa applied the brainstorming technique to this unpleasant routine? The process might go like this:

A) *Identify the problem or goal:* Kevin has to have clothes to wear to school.

B) *Come up with possible solutions* (remember, at this stage, no idea is too far out):

1. Let him wear what he already has.

2. Let him not wear anything.

3. Go to the store alone, pick out the clothes, and hog-tie him until he agrees to wear them.

4. Show him a catalog and have him pick out things he likes.

5. Teach him to sew.

6. Tell him "No school clothes, no video games."

7. Pick out the clothes, buy them, and plan to bill him when he's 18.

8. Offer to trade Kevin to the neighbors for their schnauzer.

9. (You add one) _____.

C) Review the possible solutions, choose the two or three best, and then narrow it down to one. If it doesn't work, you can always try one of the remaining options.

Looking at the choices above, Teresa might reason as follows:

1. Given the condition of last year's clothes, this option might lead people to think Kevin had been suddenly orphaned.

2. Probably not legal.

3. Has some potential, but sounds too strenuous.

4. Might work.

5. Would probably be even more frustrating than shopping.

6. Might work as a last resort.

7. An accounting nightmare.

8. Probably not legal either.

9. You decide.

If you were Teresa, where would you go from here? Which option, or combination of options, would you choose as the best? Personally, I would probably try the catalog idea, or show him a sale flyer from a local store and see if any of the back-to-school clothes advertised appealed to him. Or, I might just go to the store myself and pick out several shirts and pants, bring them home and let him look at them, then take back any he did not like.

One of the characteristics of ruts is that they are hard to climb out of. Sometimes it takes a conscious effort to break away from our fixed thinking about how something should be done. In Teresa's case, the first step in changing the back-to-school routine was to acknowledge that taking Kevin to the store to choose his clothes was not the only way to accomplish the goal.

While we don't have to go through all these steps to find ways to change unsatisfying routines, brainstorming this way can help us be creative and explore new options. (For the really knotty problems, brainstorm with a friend!) Is there a routine in your life that could benefit from some brainstorming?

Around and Around. And Around.

Remember our friend Roberta in chapter 7? Amid all the routines of her life, she had begun to feel as though she were always moving in a circle, always ending up back where she started.

Maybe she was.

We can find ways to keep from being bogged down in routines. We can build a sense of anticipation into our days. We can derive satisfaction from our daily activities and try new ways of doing things. But if we are not headed anywhere, if we have no sense of *destination*, we will still be running in circles. Even if we could eliminate every single routine from our daily lives, we still can't budge from square one if we have no place to go, no ultimate goal we want to reach.

In chapter 6 we talked about the importance of goals. Our goals give meaning to everything we do—our jobs, our family lives, our leisure activities, our times of searching and introspection. When we look at our lives from a distance (when we get out of the cornfield!), we can see whether we are, in fact, making progress toward our goals or just moving in circles.

In this and the two preceding chapters we have focused on freedom and how to keep from losing it to the forces swirling around us. Having a destination, an ultimate goal for our lives, gives our freedom meaning, too. Why do we need to be free if we have no place we want to go, anyway?

God's desire is for us to "have life, and have it to the full" (John 10:10). When our goal is to live the life God wants for us and to reflect His image in this world to the greatest extent we possibly can, then that fullness of life and that freedom can be ours.

What is your ultimate destination?

9 EXPECTATIONS: GREAT AND NOT-SO-GREAT

Recently my 11-year-old son and I had a conversation about what we were doing for dinner that night. It went like this:

Matthew: "Mom, can we eat out tonight?"

Me: "No, not tonight, because I'm fixing a nice dinner here at home."

Matthew: "Oh." (Pause) "What are we having?"

Me: "Pork chops, peas, blueberry muffins, and a fruit salad, I think."

Matthew: "Oh." (Longer pause) "C'mon, Mom, can't we have a real dinner?"

Unconventional thinker that I am, I had expected that the meal I had described would qualify as a "real" dinner, but obviously it didn't in Matthew's book. So I pursued it. So much for expectations.

Me: "What do you mean by a 'real dinner'?"

Matthew: "You know, one where we all fix our own stuff."

Me: "Oh."

* * *

My mother is an enthusiastic and creative cook. When I was growing up, dinnertime was the family's time to be together, and there was always a balanced, appealing dinner on the table. We ate it without hurrying, regardless of how much homework there was or how many other tasks needed to be done afterwards. We ate out only as a special treat.

Later on, my expectation of what dinnertime would be like in my own household was based on what I experienced as a child. My definition of a "real" dinner, historically, has been one that includes the four basic food groups, has a variety of colors and flavors, and is served in serving dishes, not in plastic containers that say "Serve by August 19." And you eat it sitting down at the table. Your body, your plate, your silverware, and your food do not leave the table until everyone has finished.

As you can imagine, the reality of dinnertime at my house has crashed head-on into this notion about how it should be. First of all, we seldom all sit down at the table at one time. Secondly, when we do eat at home, the meal generally takes about 45 minutes to fix and 15 to eat. (There's something mathematically wrong with that.) Invariably, the telephone rings while we're eating, and whoever the call is for finishes talking right about the time the others finish eating.

Sometimes we don't sit at the table at all. I have been known to fix the food, put it on the table with a stack of plates and utensils, and let each person eat whatever he wants, wherever he wants to. Another alternative, of course, is the one Matthew defined as a "real" dinner: the arrangement in which I announce that it's dinnertime and everyone fixes what he wants to eat. The four basic food groups at my house are: things that come in cans, things that don't, things that are frozen, and Twinkies.

Deep down in my heart, I know there's nothing wrong with any of these mealtime arrangements. (Well, maybe the four food groups are a little off-base.) They work for us. Our lives are busy and full, and we would rather do other things than linger over dinner. And certainly I would rather do other things than spend hours cooking. The way my mother approached dinnertime worked for those years and for the lifestyle our family had. The meal system in my household works for the way we live now.

> I remember sitting around the dinner table when I was growing up, having long discussions about politics or books or sports or current events. It wasn't unusual for us to stay at the table for two hours or more. It scares me that that kind of family life might be gone forever.
>
> —Patricia

But there is a part of me that remembers the traditional dinners in my mother's home and expects the same of me. It whispers that if I were a good mother, dinners in my home would be like that, too. It's an irrational and even silly expectation, but for some reason, when I fail to live up to it, it hurts.

What Do You Expect?

Unreasonable expectations not only cause us unnecessary hurt, frustration, and conflict, but they can also rob us of the freedom God wants us to have. They can limit our ability to develop fully the unique potential He has created in each of us. They bind us to thinking and behavior that don't fit the people we are.

Where do these unrealistic and inappropriate expectations come from? It's difficult to pinpoint all the sources, and certainly we could simply say that our expectations are shaped by "society." But let's be a little more specific, and look at three particular sources of expectations about what working mothers should be: personal history, the media, and other people.

"And the Rest Is History"

The mismatch between my expectations and reality in regard to dinnertimes is a reflection of the difference between my life as a child and my life now, between how my mother fulfilled her role and how I fulfill mine. It is unrealistic and foolish for me to think that I can simply transplant my mother's lifestyle into today and proceed as though nothing had changed in the past 30 years. The world is different. My life is different.

To illustrate vividly just how much has changed since our mothers' generation was to where we are now, try this little exercise:

Write down the year you were born. _____

Now, write down as many things as you can think of that exist today that didn't exist that year. (For example, some of the items on my list are: microwave ovens, the space shuttle, nuclear bombs, supersonic jets, diet soft drinks, the polio vaccine, AIDS, and satellite transmissions.) Write your list here:

_____   _____

_____   _____

_____   _____

_____   _____

Enough said about change. The world *is* different from what it was when our mothers were learning the ropes of motherhood.

Given the pace and the extent of change in our time, the idea of simply transplanting our mothers' lifestyle and way of doing things into this radically different world seems ludicrous. Yet many of us try in varying degrees to do just that. We try to fulfill our role as mothers in the same way the previous generation did. Then we add on another full-time job outside the home.

In other words, we try to do all those things that, based on history, we think mothers ought to do. Then on top of this schedule we spend eight or ten hours a day somewhere else, living up to a whole different set of expectations in the workplace. In the recesses of our hearts, though, we cling to expectations of motherhood that belong to another generation. What a burden to take on!

How do we resolve the conflict, then, between these expectations stemming from our personal history and the realities of our daily lives? By setting priorities and making choices.

Let's go back to the dinnertime situation. I've talked with many other mothers who experience the same discrepancy between mealtimes they knew as children and the ones in their households now, and they want to find some way to relieve the inner tension that this causes. What are our options? Here are a few:

1) We can decide that being together at dinnertime is going to be a priority in our family's lifestyle. In that case, we need our family to make a collective commitment. Adults and children alike need to avoid scheduling activities at dinnertime. Phone calls received during the meal should be returned after dinner. If we want dinnertime to be a meaningful, pleasant family time together, then it cannot be used as a dumping ground for the day's frustrations, or as a time to discipline, scold, or punish children.

2) If it's not the "family dinner" tradition that is our priority as much as simply having relaxed, pleasant times of being together, then we need to find other opportunities to build those times into our lives. Some families

enjoy going to the movies together, or to the beach, or on weekend picnics in the park, or spending Sunday afternoons at the home of good friends. Just because leisurely, sit-down dinners are a rarity at our house doesn't mean we have failed to build a sense of family togetherness. It's the *time* that counts, not the setting and not the food.

3) Compromise. Maybe we can all sit down to dinner together on Wednesday nights and Sunday afternoons, or on any two nights during the week, depending on activities. Maybe each family member will be responsible for "organizing" dinner on a different night and surprising the rest of the family with a special menu. Or maybe every other Sunday one of the children gets to suggest an activity he or she would like the family to do, even if it's just watching a rented video together or baking cookies.

If our dinnertime or our family life or our leisure time together isn't what we want it to be, that is probably because we haven't make a commitment to what we *do* want it to be. The quality of our life as a family stems from the choices we make. External forces shape that quality only when we allow them to. If we don't make choices that will bring about the quality of life we want, then by default we are letting the rest of the world make those choices for us.

The Keys to Success: Mouthwash, Cheese, and Low Heels

Living as we do in the "information age," we are constantly bombarded with messages that feed this schizophrenic way of life. Magazines, books, newspapers, movies, TV shows, and advertising all portray women in a variety of ways and give us plenty of instruction about what we ought to be doing and how. To get a glimpse of society's expectations for working women, mothers, working mothers, and women in general, we need only to look to the images created by the media.

On the one hand, these artificially created images reinforce the traditional mothering role; on the other hand, they create a stereotypical "working woman." And here we are, caught in the middle, trying to figure out who we are and what we really should be doing.

From my own observations, here are a few of the messages about working mothers you can find in the media on any given day:

- If you buy a certain brand of peanut butter, milk, mayonnaise, cheese, or toilet paper, your family will know you love them.
- If you wear high heels at the office, don't expect to get ahead.
- If you want to look brainy, wear glasses.
- Having clean, fresh-smelling clothes is of paramount importance to your loved ones. It's the least you can do for them.
- Having clean, fresh-smelling carpets is of paramount importance to your loved ones. It's the least you can do for them.
- Never appear in public unless you are fully made up and wearing clothes that match. Your "I Climbed Pike's Peak" T-shirt and University of Tulsa running shorts do not constitute an ensemble.
- Your hairdo should last all day. So should you.
- If you are overtired, or have the flu, or sprain your ankle, that's no reason to slow down. Just take XYZ pharmaceutical products and you'll be able to remain standing, and maybe even breathing, all day.
- Nothing hurts you. No demand on your time, energy, or emotion is too much. Nothing makes you sad or angry or frustrated. You can do anything. You're a working mother.
- (Your turn) _____

_____

_____

> I think sometimes we let society and the media
> tell us what we should be doing. There's just so
> much information out there, and we buy into it
> without even being aware that we're doing it.
> —Joan

In the last three weeks, not one but two women have told me what a hard decision it was for them to start wearing dresses to work instead of suits. These were both intelligent, capable, high-level professional women who were used to being in charge and making important decisions. Yet they had been so conditioned to the expectation that wearing a suit at work was somehow related to success that they had to wrestle with the decision to wear something else instead. They had bought into the stereotype of the business-suited successful woman, perhaps without even being aware of it, and had to make a specific decision to break out of that pattern. To be honest, I was proud of them both for declaring their freedom from the suit-up-for-success syndrome!

Are there any stereotypes or unrealistic images that have sneaked into your thinking and influenced your behavior? Do you need to break out of some pattern you have let enslave you?

When I taught a course in journalism to college students, the one thing I hoped they gained from the course was the ability to be critical consumers of the media—to evaluate, analyze, and scrutinize the ideas and images with which the media bombard us. I think this is doubly important for us as working mothers because there are so many images and perceptions being created about us. If we let our expectations of ourselves be set by those images, then we have relinquished control of our own thinking. That's a scary prospect. Our roles as mothers, our working lives, and our self-concepts are too important to let someone else define them for us.

Okay, Have It Your Way

Another set of expectations about how we should live our lives comes from the people around us: friends, families, coworkers, church members, and people we perceive as authority figures or role models. Often, we may respect certain people's opinions or examples in one area of their lives—say, their religious beliefs or the way they conduct themselves on the job—and inadvertently buy into their views in other areas as well without really evaluating them.

Over the years, I have worked closely with a number of talented, dedicated professional colleagues, both men and women, whose work style and accomplishments I greatly admired. For me, these individuals set the standard. I wanted, above all, to be like them, to perform on the job as effectively and creatively as they did.

Over time, though, I realized that while I could learn a great deal from them—and did—I could never make the total career commitment they had made. The priorities in my life were different. My commitment was to a balanced life in which my career was one element, not the driving force. Family, church, recreation, and physical fitness were all priorities for me, too. A totally job-centered life just wouldn't leave enough room for the other things I wanted. I could never attain the things my colleagues attained because I wasn't willing to pay the price. I had to learn to be selective about what aspects of their lives I imitated in my own.

On the other hand, I have a number of good friends who simply do not believe that mothers of small children should hold jobs outside the home. They feel that a working mother is a less-than-adequate mother. There was a time when I let myself believe they were right, and that I must be a poor mother indeed to continue my job when I had a small child at home. I let my respect and love for these individuals produce a tremendous sense of guilt. And it was only because I was letting their opinions and beliefs—instead of my own—shape my expectations.

> One of the things that's helped me a lot is giving myself the freedom to say, "Sometimes I don't like being a mother very much." For some reason, a lot of people are afraid to admit that it isn't just great all the time. It's great most of the time—but we all have our moments. I like being free to admit that.
>
> —Ava

Why are we so willing to adopt other people's expectations as our own, even when it's clear they are not right for us?

I believe one of the reasons is that we haven't had much opportunity to establish our own definitions of who and what we ought to be. There's no historical track record that tells us what works and what doesn't. There's no road map with the potholes clearly marked. We are like inventors, trying out a new invention for the first time, with no data that tell us what to expect.

So it's up to us. We have to start from scratch, defining for ourselves how we are going to live.

Two for the Price of One, or Vice Versa?

Let's begin by questioning the notion that working mothers, by definition, lead two separate lives, one at home and one at work.

I have read a number of articles that say working women should keep their "office" lives and their "personal" lives separate. There's some good sense in that approach. All of us have had the trying experience of listening to a long narrative of a coworker's domestic woes when we have a desk full of must-finish projects. And we can also attest to the unpleasant side effects of taking problems from work home with us, where they disrupt our nonworking hours.

However, there are limits to our ability to separate these two aspects of our lives. Each of us is only one person, and we are the same person whether we are at home or at work. We may dress differently, use a different vocabulary, even act differently in the two settings, but who we are remains the same. For us to constantly fight to be two people—mother and working person— means constant inner conflict and turmoil. We are trying to create two creatures out of one. In my high school zoology class, I saw one-celled animals do that, but I have yet to see a human being pull it off!

An incident involving a young woman I used to work with made it clear to me just how hard this separation is. This young woman, Terry, was an enthusiastic, energetic employee. She liked the fast-paced environment in our office and was always eager to take on new projects. She even told me one of the things she liked about her job was the constant variety and the challenge of juggling many projects at once. One week, though, it became apparent that Terry was losing her grip on the many projects she had in the works. I would ask her for work or information, and she seemed to have lost track of things. Instead of being enthusiastic as usual, she seemed oppressed and harried by the multitude of things she had to do. And yet her workload at that time was, if anything, lighter than usual.

As we were sitting in my office talking about a specific project, I casually said, "You seem to be feeling pretty pushed this week. Is there something I can do to help?"

At first she mentioned some specific projects that were not going well, and some unexpected obstacles she had encountered. Then she said, "I guess it's partly that my babysitter quit last week, and it seems like my baby has been sick constantly ever since I started this job, and the alternator on my car went out, and..."

Terry had tried hard to keep the stress in her personal life from affecting her work, but when unexpected difficulties on the job cropped up, the combination of the two was just too much to handle. Our tolerance for stress doesn't automatically double when we choose the dual role of working mother. We don't magically receive twice the patience, twice the physical stamina, twice the mental energy, or twice the normal number of hours per day.

> I think we get hung up on roles. We keep asking, "How can I combine being a mother with a career?" when what we should be asking is, "What unique and special contribution can I make to this world?"
>
> —Joan

As much as we would like to think we are a generation of superwomen, with strength and abilities far beyond those of mortal creatures, we're not. Yet we try to fulfill the mothering role in the same way women did 30 or 40 years ago, and then we take on a full-time job outside the home and expect it not to make any difference in how we perform as mothers. Isn't that demanding more of ourselves than is realistic or even possible?

If we dispense with the idea that our roles as mothers and working persons should be separate, where does that leave us? Do we take our babies to the office or meet with customers over our kitchen tables? Of course not. It simply means that we define ourselves as persons, not as characters playing roles at home and at work. We go back to the question "Who am I?" instead of starting with the question "What am I?"

Once we have developed in our own minds a clear picture of who we are, then we can stop defining ourselves by the things we do. We can then view motherhood, work, and all other aspects of our lives as part of an integrated whole, not as separate components of a fragmented existence.

Try this: Imagine that you are looking at yourself through a specially made set of binoculars that can see two completely different images. One side of the binoculars shows you on the job; the other side shows you at home with your family. Picture the two images the binoculars show. Where are you in each one? How are you dressed? Who is with you? What are you doing? Be specific about each image.

Now imagine that you are adjusting the focus on the binoculars so that the two images merge, and there is only one. This is you—a whole, integrated person. Picture what the image looks like now. Where are you? What are you doing? What does the expression on your face reflect?

This little exercise is just a way to focus our thinking on the idea of "oneness," to help us stop viewing ourselves as women living dual lives. Now let's explore the many dimensions of that single image.

"I'm A Designer Original!"

In previous chapters we looked at the fact that God created each of us lovingly and individually as a reflection of Him. We talked about His continuing interest in us and His concern for our well-being. We know He loves and cares about us. The Bible also tells us that He has given each of us a special combination of gifts—talent, personality, skill, ability—that equips us to fill a role in this world that no one else can fill. And that's the only role that really matters, because as we seek to fill that "master role," the other things we do will fall into place.

> *So do not worry, saying "What shall we eat?"*
> *or "What shall we drink?" or "What shall we*
> *wear?" For the pagans run after all these things,*
> *and your heavenly Father knows that you need*
> *them. But seek first his kingdom and his*
> *righteousness, and all these things will be given*
> *to you as well.*
>
> —*Jesus*
> *(in Matthew 6:31-33)*

The people of Jesus' time were concerned about God's expectations of them. They asked Jesus to tell them the most important things God wanted them to do. The answer He gave them is as true today as it was then. "Love the Lord your God with all your heart and with all your soul and with all your mind," He told them, and "Love your neighbor as yourself" (Matthew 22:37-39).

The Bible spells out God's expectations of us. He makes clear the kind of lives He wants us to live. When our focus is on being the *people* He wants us to be, then we will be the kind of mothers, workers, spouses, friends, and citizens He wants us to be also. No matter how many roles we fulfill, we will still be centered in His loving concern. I believe the ultimate freedom lies in that knowledge.

God's Expectations

Lord, what do You want me to do?

What are your expectations of me?

To care about that old-fashioned idea called "righteousness";

To make my life choices and my day-to-day decisions with integrity and compassion;

To be truthful and constructive in the things I say, and not use the power of words to hurt other people;

To treat others fairly and respectfully, knowing You created each of them with love, just as You did me;

To recognize evil when I see it, and to follow the example of people who love and honor You;

To keep my promises, both to You and to other people, even when it's hard to do;

To give of myself, my time, my talent, my resources generously, without demanding a high return;

Never to let the prospect of material or personal gain make me compromise what I know is right;

I know that if I do these things, nothing can conquer me, because You will sustain me.

(Based on Psalm 15)

10 THE BALANCING ACT

Picture one of those old-fashioned scales, the kind with two shallow, circular pans hanging at the ends of two arms balanced on a fulcrum. You have a set of little metal slugs of specific weights. You put what you want to weigh in one of the pans, then you add weights to the other until the two pans are in balance. If you put, say, a handful of feathers in one pan, and a ten-pound weight in the other, THUNK! The pan with the weight in it crashes down. No balance there.

Have there been times when your life felt so out of balance that you could almost hear the THUNK?

I've been known to let my life get so unbalanced that if there's a breeze I'll tip over and fall into a hole.

—Sarah

Balance. It's what keeps our lives on an even keel. It gives us stability; it enables us to move forward instead of zigzagging from side to side, from one extreme to another. It keeps us from going so far off course that we end up somewhere we don't want to be.

113

A working mother's life is often described as a juggling act, and with good reason. We juggle an ever-changing assortment of priorities, demands, and needs, and the challenge is to keep them in balance. We are like the man in the circus who stacks 25 china plates and then balances them on his head. If his balance falters, it's not a pretty sight.

Look at the list below of paired factors that working mothers have to keep in balance. Suppose you were given a scale, like the one described above, and a set of ten equal weights. Your assignment: For each pair in the list below, divide the ten weights between the two sides of the scale to reflect how well-balanced you feel the items are in your life.

For example, if I feel I have a good balance between meeting my own needs and meeting my family's needs, I would assign five weights to each. If I tend to be a work-aholic and don't do a very good job of balancing work and family, I might assign seven weights to work and only three to family. Remember, this exercise is to give you a picture of how things really are, not how you think they should be or would like them to be. (Note: Things can be in balance without having equal amounts of time or energy devoted to them. If you spend more hours at work than at leisure activities, that doesn't mean they are out of balance. This exercise focuses on the *balance*, not on the actual amount of time or energy devoted to the activity.)

Here's the list:

# of weights	# of weights
____ Caring for other people	____ Caring for self
____ Worrying	____ Problem-solving

___ Work-related
activities

___ Non-work-related
activities

___ Children's physical
needs

___ Children's emotional
needs

___ Children's intellec-
tual/academic needs

___ Children's spiritual
needs

___ Family activities

___ Activities with
people other than
family

___ Busy times

___ Quiet times

___ Professional/job
growth

___ Personal/spiritual
growth

___ Chores ("have-to-
do's")

___ Fun

___ Seriousness

___ Laughter

___ Giving

___ Receiving

___ New skills/ideas/
experiences

___ Existing skills/ideas/
experiences

___ Repetition/routine

___ Variety/change

What other elements or considerations can you think of that working mothers are required to balance? Add them here, and assign a number of weights to each.

# of weights

# of weights

___ _____

___ _____

___ _____

___ _____

___ _____

___ _____

We could probably spend the next week listing more and more factors that working mothers have to juggle. One of the ongoing challenges of learning to be a whole person is finding ways to keep the various aspects of our lives in balance. Often, just when we get one set of elements to balance out, another one goes THUNK!

If this exercise has given you a bird's-eye view of some specific balances in your life, you might consider whether you want to make some changes in areas that you have identified as being out of balance. First, review the items you rated in the list above as being in good balance, and pat yourself on the back for your successful juggling! Now, if you want to give some thought to those areas that seem out of balance, take a moment to zero in on one or two of them and consider some changes you might make. What would help you achieve better balance in those areas? Adjusting your schedule to allow more time for a certain type of activity? Changing your "thinking routines" as described in chapter 8? Making a concerted effort to build more of a certain quality into your life?

THE FOUR BASIC BALANCES

We are all called upon to juggle a great many things, to achieve and maintain an infinite number of delicate balances. In the exercise above we looked at some very specific balances that affect our day-to-day living. I believe, though, that there are four fundamental balances—much more critical even than those listed above—we must maintain in our lives. They are:

1. Freedom and commitment
2. Self and other people
3. Doing and being
4. The lasting and the temporary

Without balance in those four areas, we will continually face frustration and confusion. Not only will we find it difficult to cope with the demands on us as working mothers without balance in these four areas, but we will also find it virtually impossible to achieve a sense of wholeness as human beings.

Balancing Freedom and Commitment

> If you're talking about relationships and commitments, I think being "free" probably just means being lonely.
>
> —Corinne

If our freedom were simply a total absence of any restraints—no attachments, no rules, no responsibility, no values—then life would be meaningless indeed. That kind of freedom isn't really freedom at all. It's a vacuum; it's emptiness. That's not the kind of freedom God gives us.

The freedom God intends for us is not so much freedom *from* as freedom *to*. Freedom to live the full life He wants for us; to be the whole, unique individuals He created us to be. That freedom can only be realized when we balance it with a twofold commitment: 1) commitment to living by His guidelines and 2) commitment to fulfilling the unique role He has for us in this world, whether in relation to our families, our jobs, our society, our church, or our country.

Jesus told us, "If you hold to my teaching, you are really my disciples. Then you will know the truth, and the truth will set you free" (John 8:31,32). How does that work? How does knowing the truth set us free?

In the preceding chapters we have looked at some of the factors that can erode our sense of freedom: outdated perceptions, unrealistic expectations, pointless routines, artificial limitations. There are plenty of other forces, both within and outside us, that can jeopardize our freedom, too. Some of them are: ambition that seeks success at any cost; an unyielding desire for power or material wealth; relationships, sexual or otherwise, that hurt and destroy rather than enhance our personhood; jealousy of other people's good fortune or achievements; consuming absorption with some single aspect of our lives such as our children or our work; and bigotry, anger, or hatred.

> *Live as free men, but do not use freedom as a*
> *cover-up for evil; live as servants of God*
> *(1 Peter 2:16).*

These forces, like the things we described in the preceding chapters, are enslavers. When these destructive traits gain a foothold in our lives, they soon begin to dictate the choices and decisions we make. They rob us of our freedom. A person whose life is ruled by greed or ambition isn't free. A person whose relationships are based on potential advantage isn't free. A person who lets herself be consumed by roles and the expectations of others isn't free.

Knowing the truth—that is, knowing God's master design for His world and the principles He established for it—protects us from enslavement by the destructive forces around and within us. We still have to deal with them, but we do not have to be subjugated by them.

For working mothers, knowing the simple truth that God created us with special, individual gifts to contribute to this world frees us from the need to be defined by what we do—our jobs, our parenting, our social or civic achievements. At the same time, it represents a commitment to carrying out our responsibilities in the very best way we can, always attempting to do what we know is right in His eyes.

Unless you have a great deal more fortitude than I do, I will bet there are days when a little voice inside you mutters, "Being a mother is too tough for me. I don't have the wisdom, the patience, the stamina, the juggling skills, or the emotional endurance this job requires. Can I quit?"

But we don't quit. Motherhood is a commitment. We forge ahead because we have been entrusted with an infinitely important job to do. Our ancient friend the psalmist wrote in Psalm 15 that a person who pleases God is one who "keeps his oath even when it hurts" (15:4). Sometimes being a working mother hurts—like when you have to leave your 12-year-old at home alone with a cold, tucked under a blanket on the sofa, because you can't miss a meeting at work. Or when you're doling out discipline and it literally hurts you more than it does your child. The hurting is part of the package.

What if you could wave a magic wand and suddenly be free of all your commitments: no work demands, no parenting responsibilities, no marriage vows, no family needs, no friendships requiring time and effort, and best of all, no do's and don'ts for living. Wow, freedom! Terrific, huh?

Not really, of course. No small hands clutching yours. No gleeful "Mommy!" when you show up at the day care center at the end of the day. No one to say "I understand" or "We all make mistakes" or "You're the best." No way to know right from wrong, or to tell a wise choice from a foolish one. No sense of your place in a very big world.

Freedom without commitment is emptiness. Commitment without freedom is enslavement. How fortunate we are that God enables us to have balance.

Balancing Self and Other People

Vicki admits to being a "fixer."

"I just can't help it," she says. "When I see someone who's having problems, or who's hurting—someone at work, or a neighbor, or a friend of a friend—before I know it I'm running around, doing this and that, trying to 'fix' whatever the problem is.

"What happens is I end up spending a lot of time listening to people's problems, trying to give them advice, or taking care of them in some way. And I keep saying to myself over and over, 'What else can I do that will help them?' "

Vicki's husband finally made this observation to her: "You know, I've watched you do this a lot of times now: You not only use up a lot of time and energy doing things to help—which is great—but you also take on the other person's pain. I see you actually hurting because you've become so involved in what they're going through. It seems like you just multiply the pain.

"Or else you take on so much activity on someone else's behalf that you just create more stress for yourself because there isn't enough time for everything. Isn't there a way you can do some things to help without creating problems for yourself in the process? I think you need to admit to yourself that there are limits to what you can do for someone else."

Are you a fixer, too?

Don't be afraid to come out of the closet. It's okay. Our world would be a sad, cold, and lonely place without its fixers.

Being a mother means being a fixer to some extent. We grow so accustomed to supporting, nurturing, understanding, consoling, and doing things for other people—fixing—that whether or not we are, like Vicki, fixers by nature, we end up in that role.

Being a fixer has its rewards. There is satisfaction in knowing you've helped someone. Particularly when our own self-esteem is low, it feels good to do something and know that it's valuable and appreciated. Certainly the Bible encourages us repeatedly to "look not only to [our] own interests, but also to the interests of others" (Philippians 2:4) and to care for the needy. Fixers are often the ones who are willing to meet other people's needs when no one else will. The work of churches, community service agencies, international relief organizations, and the helping professions would cease to exist without fixers.

Fixers run a risk, though: the risk of losing the balance between the needs of self and the needs of other people. For working mothers, with the wide variety of needs and demands they deal with every day, the risk is especially high.

One longtime fixer who realized her life was severely out of balance described it this way:

"I began to feel as though if I looked in the mirror there wouldn't be anyone there. I had so totally devoted myself to meeting other people's needs and expectations that there literally wasn't anything left of me. I became a nonperson. The only identity I had was in the things I did for other people."

Being a lifelong fixer myself—and proud of it!—I'd be the last to say fixers should stop fixing. But I do believe we can structure our efforts for maximum effectiveness and minimal risk of losing our balance. For example, we can:

Choose carefully. In any given situation, there are things we can do most effectively and things that other individuals can handle better. There's no point in volunteering to keep a friend's three children while she visits her invalid mother if your own day-care situation is already a mess and your one bathroom is being remodeled. Instead, offering to handle your friend's mail, make telephone calls, feed the dog, or take the kids out for a day makes a lot more sense.

Admit our limitations. It's painful to see someone grieving over the death of a loved one or the end of a marriage or the loss of a job. In that situation, the fixer asks herself, "What can I do to help?" The reality is that grief, anger, and hurt have to run their course, and while we can do some small tasks to make day-to-day life easier for the person, we can't do much to relieve the pain. Internalizing it so that we suffer, too, doesn't help the other person; it only makes us less effective.

The same is true of our children's heartaches. Being rejected by friends, being laughed at, being disappointed in outcomes, being hurt in romantic relationships—they all go with growing up. Because we are mothers, we would give anything to fix the pain, but we can't. What we can do is help the healing process along with love and understanding.

Remember to care for ourselves. My late father once described my mother as a person of "vast inner resources." We can't give to other people if we let our own inner resources be depleted.

God understands that we need renewal and replenishment if we are to give of ourselves to other people. He knows that, unlike Him, we don't have infinite resources of love, compassion, patience, understanding, insights, wisdom, and all those other things we need as mothers and as human beings. We run low. Sometimes we run out. Sometimes we feel that if we have to give one more iota of nurturing or support, the cupboard of our hearts will be bare. We will have used up all our inner resources.

The Bible contains many illustrations of how God provides for renewal and replenishment of our spirits. One of my favorites is a story in the New Testament in which Jesus meets a woman who has come to the town's well to draw water for her household. Jesus tells her, "Everyone who drinks this water will be thirsty again, but whoever drinks the water I give him will never thirst" (John 4:13). When we rely on God as the source of our inner strength, the well will never run dry. The psalmist says we will be "like a tree planted by streams of water, which yields its fruit in season and whose leaf does not wither" (1:3). Through prayer, through the reading of His Word, through the example of people of wisdom and faith, we draw on God's infinite resources—and thereby replenish our own.

Once we develop the habit of drawing from the well of God's "living water," we find that we can give away more and more of ourselves without feeling emptied. "He who refreshes others will himself be refreshed" (Proverbs 11:25) is the promise God makes to us.

There are other little ways we can renew our spirits on a day-to-day basis, too, by finding opportunities for laughter, for friendship, for giving, for enjoying some small pleasure, or just for fun. If we're like Kathy, our enthusiastic runner in chapter 3, it may be a sport or exercise that makes us feel refreshed. Or maybe it's just getting together with a good friend or watching a child perform in a school program.

Recently I met with a group of women from my church to talk about some of the concerns of working mothers. The stimulating discussion, the mutual support within the group, and the reassurance that we all share common problems made me feel recharged and renewed.

Another time, I was in a meeting with four other women at work. We went over the first several agenda items in an efficient and businesslike way. Then, for some reason, one of the women mentioned something funny that had happened in the office earlier that day. Another person made a comment about it, and before we knew it we were all making absolutely ridiculous remarks and laughing so hard that we were mopping tears off our faces. How refreshing it was just to be totally *silly*. May we never outgrow our ability to enjoy the ridiculous!

What is there in your life that gives your heart a lift? Music? An absolutely terrific book? A really hard work-out? Getting together with friends over a pizza and swapping tales of "life's most embarrassing moments"?

Just because a friend or loved one needs us—which is virtually all the time, in one way or another—doesn't mean we stop being persons ourselves. It isn't suddenly against the rules to attend to our own needs whether the need is for laughter, for inspiration, for love, for relaxation, or for support. Jesus told us to love our neighbors as ourselves. That's balance. Fixers, take heed.

Balancing Doing and Being

"She's a real go-getter."

"You want to get something done, ask a busy person."

"She's a person who can always be counted on to get the job done."

Our world loves doers.

Much of what you have read so far in this book has been about the balance between doing and being. Defining ourselves by our jobs, our families, or by other "doing-oriented" roles and contexts instead of as persons throws off this balance. So does trying to meet other people's expectations when they are inappropriate for us. So does trying to give ourselves value by "fixing" other people's lives until we are burnt out. All these approaches place disproportionate emphasis on doing and not enough on being.

Doing is necessary to functioning in the world we live in. We can't sit around all day contemplating our existence! The things we do can give us a sense of accomplishment, usefulness, and self-esteem; they can bring us rewards, too—paychecks, recognition, and satisfaction. The imbalance occurs only when we begin to believe that our self-worth lies entirely in what we do and not in who we are.

We are children of God. "It is he who made us, and we are his; we are his people, the sheep of his pasture" (Psalm 100:3). We are the creatures to whom He chose to give dominion over all the rest of His creation. He made us "a little lower than the heavenly beings" and crowned us "with glory and honor" (Psalm 8:5). We don't have to earn His love; in fact, we can't. We have only to accept it and to acknowledge His sovereignty in our lives. Because we're human, it isn't possible for us to be good enough to earn God's love. Only Jesus lived that kind of perfect life. What a relief to know God loves us unconditionally.

Once we accept that unconditional love, we can stop running around trying to earn worthiness or to create some justification for our being in this world. The fact that He has put us here is enough. That's the being part. The doing part is seeking to live the lives He wants for us and to fill that place He's reserved for us alone—or, as Joan put it in chapter 9, to make that "unique and special contribution" in this world.

Balancing the Lasting and the Temporary

Several years ago when a hurricane passed near the west coast of Florida, the winds and waves it stirred up caused widespread flooding in the state. My husband and I were out of town that day; we returned to find our house—our dream house that we had worked so hard for—awash in murky, foul-smelling salt water. Anything on or near the floor was thoroughly waterlogged; our appliances and furniture were damaged, and some ruined; books and pictures that had been stored in cupboards near the floor were destroyed.

Naturally, we couldn't stay in the house; we had to live with friends until the cleanup had progressed enough for us to move back in.

And we were among the lucky ones. Our son, who had stayed with a babysitter, was safe and sound. None of our friends or family members had been hurt. Some families' homes had been washed out from under them; people had been injured and some killed.

The experience was a crash course in what's lasting and what isn't.

The process of cleaning up took several weeks, and it was months before our life seemed back to normal. But long after that—in fact, even now—I still remember the feeling I had then of being stripped of my possessions, robbed of the things I had worked for and treasured. I couldn't escape a new awareness of the temporary nature of those things.

> *Do not store up for yourselves treasures on earth, where moth and rust destroy, and where thieves break in and steal. But store up for yourselves treasures in heaven, where moth and rust do not destroy, and where thieves do not break in and steal. For where your treasure is, there your heart will be also.*
> —*Jesus*
> *(Matthew 6:19-21)*

Those of us who work outside the home spend a great deal of our time in the business world. That world has its own set of rules, values, and rewards. The ultimate reward is success, defined in terms of more money, a loftier title, a bigger office, more prestige, more influence.

Unfortunately, any of those things can disappear in an instant. The company can falter, the management can "clean house," an illness or disability can put an end to a promising career. Just like the possessions damaged and destroyed in the flood, the outward rewards of the working world are temporary.

"Do not wear yourself out to get rich," the writer of Proverbs says, "have the wisdom to show restraint. Cast but a glance at riches, and they are gone, for they will surely sprout wings and fly off to the sky like an eagle" (23:4,5).

That doesn't mean we can't enjoy the rewards of our hard work, both the material rewards and the intangible rewards of challenge and accomplishment. After all, God gives us the ability to obtain them. It's keeping the balance that is important.

How then do we "store up treasures in heaven"? By investing ourselves, our abilities, and our resources in the things that do last: the values we pass on to our children and the paths we set them on; the contributions we make to changing the world for the better; the influence we can have as people of integrity, compassion, and faith.

> *Now faith is being sure of what we hope for and certain of what we do not see (Hebrews 11:1).*

We store up treasures in heaven when we accept the reality of God even though we cannot see Him, and when we acknowledge that there are lasting values different from those set by the business world, the media, or society.

Only when we keep our eyes on "what we do not see," when we focus on those values beyond the visible, the material, and the comfortable, can we restore and maintain the balance.

Where are your treasures stored?

11 MORE PRECIOUS THAN RUBIES: ME!
Let's Build the Best

Let's imagine that you have been assigned to a small, hand-picked committee charged with the task of creating the ideal working mother. The sciences of robotics, genetics, and cellular biology have progressed at warp speed, and it is now possible to engineer human beings to preselected specifications.

Expense is no object. You can use any information and any kind of material you wish.

To help you in your task, each member of the committee has been given a set of worksheets, which are reproduced below. The worksheets need to be completed before the committee's next meeting.

Worksheet #1: Raw Materials

Instructions: In this worksheet, we are going to identify the qualities and the abilities our ideal working mother needs. This list will then serve as a blueprint to help us carry out the rest of the project.

Rank the items in the list below according to how important you think they are for a working mother to have. Rank the most important quality as #1, the next most important as #2, etc. If you think two or more qualities are equally important, go ahead and assign them the same rank. Leave out of your ranking the ones you don't think are needed at all. Use the spaces at the end of the list to add any further qualities or abilities you think are important.

Qualities

_____ patience

_____ sense of humor

_____ organization

_____ compassion

_____ self-control

_____ a sense of personhood

_____ tolerance for soap scum, pet odors, and grimy fingerprints

_____ sensitivity to the needs of other people

_____ a sense of self-worth

_____ a grasp on reality

_____ a positive view of the world

_____ a high tolerance for frustration

_____ high energy

_____ knowledge of how long any given food can be kept in the refrigerator before changing color

_____ acceptance of being imperfect

_____ wisdom

_____ a clear set of values—spiritual, moral, ethical

_____ a willingness to learn, grow, and change

_____ _____

_____ _____

_____ _____

_____ _____

_____ _____

Abilities

_____ ability to see the good in people and situations

_____ ability to do what is right when something else would be easier

_____ ability to learn from experience, both her own and other people's

_____ ability to repeat a request like "Please wipe your feet" four times in five minutes without losing her temper

_____ ability to see past difficulties and keep them in perspective

_____ ability to make decisions without second-guessing them later

_____ ability to say both "yes" and "no," and to know which is best in any given situation

_____ ability to laugh

_____ ability to relax

_____ ability to think like a child

_____ ability to see things from another person's viewpoint

_____ ability to do things to meet her own needs without feeling guilty

_____ ability to accept limitations in herself and others

_____ ability to put on makeup in the car

_____ ability to listen intently to a lengthy story about Peter's new gerbil while driving in six lanes of traffic

_____ ability to experience joy and wonder

_____ ability to say "I'm sorry; I was wrong."

_____ ability to say "I don't know."

_____ ability to answer the phone, dish up chili, feed the dog, and stuff celery simultaneously

_____ ability to forgive herself when she makes a mistake or displeases someone else

_____ ability to develop and maintain friendships

_____ ability to derive satisfaction from her accomplishments, big and small

_____ _____

_____ _____

_____ _____

_____ _____

_____ _____

_____ _____

_____ _____

_____ _____

Worksheet #2: Resources

Instructions: Now that we know some of the characteristics we want our ideal working mother to have, we need to know where to look for the ingredients to concoct her. Since we want her to be a real person, not a robot, we're going to look for those ingredients in the people around us instead of in a test tube or a bionics lab.

In the spaces below, list a particular "ingredient" or characteristic, and then list the person you know who best represents that quality. Use the lists of qualities and abilities for reference if you like.

(To get you started, I have listed some of my suggested "ingredients.")

Ingredient	Source
Sense of humor	My friend Connie, the only adult I know who still makes funny faces
Creativity	My cousin Judy, who thinks up the most amazing and fun things for children to do
Ability to think like a child	Connie again. She has an uncanny knack for seeing things from a child's point of view
Perspective on work	Pat, who says, "A job is a job. It's not my life; it's just one part of my life."

Your turn:

_____   _____

_____   _____

_____   _____

_____   _____

_____   _____

Now continue with this worksheet by listing the very best qualities in *you*, the ones that should be included in the ideal working mother. Then take a moment to appreciate the good things about yourself.

_____

_____

_____

_____

_____

_____

_____

Discovering the Model

Building the ideal working mother is a tough assignment. As we have learned from the worksheets above, just putting together the list of "raw materials" is a challenge in itself.

But isn't that the assignment we make to ourselves every day? Aren't we trying to build that ideal creature out of the raw materials allotted to us—our own unique combination of characteristics and circumstances?

Certainly each of us wants to fulfill her many complex roles in the best way possible, and yet there's remarkably little out there to guide us. We look in vain for the perfect role model: that woman who has woven the many strands of her life into a serviceable fabric—one that looks attractive, stretches easily, and stands up to everyday wear and tear!

Believe it or not, there is such a role model. The blueprint for the ideal working mother does exist. On the following page is a description of her, based on that blueprint.

At last! Somebody has finally described the person we working mothers strive to be. Doesn't it feel good to know that someone recognizes who we are and what we are trying to accomplish?

Actually, this particular blueprint has been around since approximately 400 B.C. (Surprise!) Its original version appears in the Bible as the thirty-first chapter of the Book of Proverbs. This version is my own paraphrase.

The chapter that is the basis for the passage above was written over 2300 years ago, yet it speaks to us as though it were written exclusively for our generation of working mothers. God really does understand our needs and circumstances today. Let's take a closer look at this description of the ideal working mother found in Proverbs 31.

Portrait of A Working Mother

The working mother is truly a treasure.

She is more precious than the most valuable gems.

Her family, friends, employer, and coworkers trust and depend on her.

She has a positive influence on those around her.

She works hard and carries out her responsibilities conscientiously.

She's careful in her decisions, whether in business, financial, or personal matters.

She approaches tasks with energy and enthusiasm, and avoids wasted time and effort.

She's not afraid to pitch in when a job needs to be done.

Even though she's constantly busy, she cares about people in need and finds meaningful ways to help them.

Because she plans ahead whenever she can and tries to be prepared for what's around the corner,

She doesn't have to spend time worrying about the future.

She is a person of inner strength and outward dignity.

When she talks, her words are careful and wise; people know they can respect and rely on what she says.

She stays on top of what's going on in her household; she knows how to relax, but she isn't lazy.

Her children love and look up to her; her spouse and other loved ones know she's something special.

Outward appearance can be deceiving, but this working mother's beauty comes from the inside.

She tries to live the life God wants for her, and she is precious to Him; her goal is to do what's right in His eyes.

May the world recognize her worth and give her the praise she deserves!

1. She has a "rightness" of spirit.

The quality of her character makes this woman stand out from others. The King James Version calls her "a virtuous woman"; the New International Version calls her "a wife of noble character." She is a person who cares about doing the right thing, and because of that she is precious to others and makes a valuable contribution to the world. In short, "She is worth far more than rubies" (verse 10).

2. She brings good to others.

Although the Bible presents this woman as a wife, her qualities aren't confined to the marriage relationship. The Bible says "Her husband has full confidence in her and . . . she brings him good, not harm, all the days of her life" (verses 11, 12). Surely other people can depend on her just as her husband does, and count on her to focus on what is good in them and in the world.

3. She's a good juggler of time and effort.

The woman described in Proverbs 31 is, like all of us, a juggler of roles and responsibilities. Specifically, the Bible says her tasks include spinning and weaving, shopping for groceries "from afar," preparing the food for her household, and sewing her family's clothing and linens. She not only runs her household, but she runs a business, too:

> *She makes linen garments and sells them, and*
> *supplies the merchants with sashes*
> *(Proverbs 31:24).*

She's a working mother in every sense of the word. To get all these things done, she even "gets up while it is still dark!"

A woman with this many responsibilities is not only willing to work hard, but she is also able to work efficiently, to get the most out of the time and effort she invests in any given task.

She's a woman who takes her responsibilities seriously because she knows other people depend on her. That's part of the reason her friends, family, and coworkers know she can be counted on.

4. She makes decisions carefully.

The Bible tells us she "considers a field and buys it; out of her earnings she plants a vineyard.... She sees that her trading is profitable, and her lamp does not go out at night" (verses 16-18).

She thinks before she makes decisions. She plans. She isn't impulsive in important matters. She has a good measure of common sense and knows when to use it.

5. She remembers that others are in need.

As we try to squeeze our many commitments into a mere 24 hours a day, it can be very easy to forget that there is a hurting, hungry, needy world out there. Not only our time, but our energy, too, is limited. Yet we have so much to give—our talent, our compassion, our specialized skills and know-how. Somewhere in her busy schedule, our ideal working mother "opens her arms to the poor and extends her hands to the needy" (verse 20).

6. She acts instead of worrying about the future.

Worrying saps our energy, frays our nerves, and doesn't solve problems. The woman of Proverbs 31 looks ahead, takes the measures she can to deal with what is down the road, and then moves on instead of fretting and stewing and standing still.

> *When it snows, she has no fear for her*
> *household; for all of them are clothed in*
> *scarlet.... She can laugh at the days to come*
> *(Proverbs 31:21, 25).*

7. *Her inner qualities show in her outward behavior.*

One of the illustrations Jesus used frequently in His preaching was the idea that you can tell the quality of a tree by the fruit it bears. Healthy trees, rooted in good soil, bear good fruit. Trees that are damaged or unhealthy, or rooted in poor soil, produce poor fruit. People, He pointed out, are the same way. Their outward behavior—their "fruit"— reveals their character.

Our role model in Proverbs 31 "is clothed with strength and dignity" (verse 25). Everything about her—her actions, her words, even her manner and bearing—reveal a strong and sound character. The things she says and does are in keeping with the values she believes in.

"Charm is deceptive, and beauty is fleeting; but a woman who fears the Lord is to be praised" (verse 30). We can't all look like models or movie stars. Age, illness, even a car accident can change our outward appearance overnight or over time. If our beauty is only on the outside, it simply won't last. What lasts is a beauty of spirit that is anchored in timeless values and unchanging truths.

8. *She chooses her words carefully.*

One of the things I have learned as I have moved from job to job is that when you are the new person on the work team, you have to earn the right to be heard. The new employee who breezes into the office and immediately starts to talk as though she knows all the answers—when she can't possibly, because she hasn't been there long enough—earns only skepticism and negative feelings. The person who listens carefully, collects information, thinks things over, and then speaks is the one whose opinion is valued and even sought. People know they can learn from her.

The same principle applies in dealing with our children. It is easy to simply say the first thing that comes into our heads. But I find that then, more often than not, we have to backtrack later. Making threats is a good example of this. "If you don't clean up your room, you can't go to Tony's to play this afternoon" is fine until you realize that you were counting on a quiet afternoon of reading while your son was at Tony's. Who ends up being punished?

When I tell my son things, I want them to be right and valuable. I want my words to communicate to him the values I love. I want my words to help him find joy in the world around him and to respond to the good in other people. Useless threats, bigoted generalizations, sarcastic remarks, and unkind comments about other people will not achieve those goals. I only hope that, part of the time at least, I can learn to "speak with wisdom."

9. *Others respect her.*

People are quick to spot phonies. It doesn't take long for other people to see through insincerity, shallowness, and manipulation. Abraham Lincoln was so right when he pointed out that we can't fool everyone all the time.

Our ideal working mother is respected because people know that what you see is what you get. They know she will be honest with them and that they can trust her; they know that, even though they may disagree with her, she will stick by the principles she believes in.

10. *Her children look up to her.*

"Her children arise and call her blessed" says the Bible. What a wonderful image! To be praised by your children must surely be one of the most heartwarming experiences a mother could possibly have.

A few years ago my mother visited my adult Sunday school class with me. She sat down next to my friend Gail, and in the few minutes before the class started, they had a chance to become acquainted.

A few days later I was having lunch with Gail. "I really enjoyed talking with your mother in Sunday school," she said. "How fortunate you are to have grown up with a mother like that!"

Naturally, I passed Gail's comment along to my mother, knowing it would please her. Gail was able to sense what it would be like to be my mother's daughter, and she felt that it must be a real privilege—which indeed it is. She put into words what I have long known, but probably not often enough expressed.

As I reflect on that sentiment, that feeling of being privileged to have the mother God gave me, I wonder what I could do over the years that would make my son feel that way about having me for a mother. Perhaps I need to reflect on my own childhood and learn from my mother's example.

I asked some other mothers what they would most like their children, as adults looking back on childhood, to say about them. Here are some of the responses:

Just that I loved them without reservation.
　　　　　　　　　　　　　　　　—Karen

That I gave them a sense of specialness.
　　　　　　　　　　　　　　　　—Louann

I'd want them to say that they respected me, and that they were always sure of my unconditional love.　　　　　　　　　　—Sylvia

That I was fun-loving.　　　　　　—Ava

That I helped them learn to like themselves.
　　　　　　　　　　　　　　　　—Pat

That my actions backed up my words.
　　　　　　　　　　　　　　　　—Linda

That I gave them a sense of trust and security so they knew that, no matter what happened, they could always come back.　　　—Joan

After the Blueprint, the Building

Living up to the role model we have just studied should keep us busy for the rest of our lives! How refreshing it is, though, to have a sense of direction, a road map to help us choose our "destination" as working mothers.

Are you ready to take on a major challenge? Are you ready to map out some new goals for yourself?

Here's the challenge: Commit to a ten-week plan of soul-searching and reflection. Each week for ten weeks, focus on one of the qualities of the ideal working mother as described above. During the week think about where you are in relation to that quality. Ask yourself some questions to help you decide if you want and/or need to make changes in that area, and what those changes might be. Acknowledge your strengths and be patient as you try to improve your weaknesses.

There is a simple chart below to help you with this ten-week project. To make it a personal challenge, put your name in the blank at the beginning of each sentence in the chart.

As you work through the chart, refer to the two worksheets at the beginning of this chapter and transfer any information from them to the chart to help you set goals in each area and decide what changes you might want to make.

Yes, this is an ambitious commitment. But think of the rewards! Following through on these ten steps will teach you volumes about the person that you are, not just in relation to work and to your family, but in the total context of your life. It will give you a chance to think about your values, your strengths, your weak spots, your decision-making habits, your relationships. It can be as comprehensive or as specific as you want it to be.

God gives us incredible potential. Use this exercise as a chance to explore the uncharted depths of the unique and amazing creature He has made: *you.*

Week 1:   **Date** _____

_____ *has a "rightness" of spirit.*

How do I determine what is right? What basic values guide my decisions? In the majority of situations, do I genuinely try to do the right thing, or do I more often choose what's easiest or most convenient? If I had to, could I clearly state the basic criteria that I use for identifying right and wrong?

Week 2:   **Date** _____

_____ *brings good to other people.*

Looking over the last week, what are some examples of instances in which I brought good to other people? Are there some people I have trouble viewing in a positive light or treating in a positive way? What does it really mean to me to "bring good to other people"?

Week 3:   **Date** _____

_____ *is a good juggler of time and effort.*

Do I get the most out of the time and effort I spend on any given task? Do I generally approach a task vigorously or halfheartedly? Are there some tasks I could handle more efficiently? Am I willing to accept responsibility for the end product?

Week 4:   **Date** _____

_____ *makes decisions carefully.*

What process do I use to make decisions? What values guide my choices? (See Week 1 above.) Do I tend to let irrelevant or unimportant considerations enter into my decisions? On the whole, what proportion of my decisions in any given area of my life turn out to be good ones? What could I do to improve my "batting average"?

Week 5:   **Date** _____

_____ *remembers that others are in need.*

What contributions do I regularly make to the needs of people outside my own circle of family and friends? What specific talents, skills, or gifts could I use to help other people?

Week 6:   **Date** _____

_____ *acts instead of worrying about the future.*

Am I a worrier? What events or situations cause me the most worry? What actions could I take that would enable me to worry less and feel more at peace about these areas? How could I become more disciplined when I feel myself starting to worry?

Week 7:   **Date** _____

_____'s *inner qualities show in her outward behavior.*

Looking back on the things I did yesterday, what qualities did I demonstrate by those actions? What qualities do I *want* people to see in me, based on my actions? How could I better demonstrate those qualities?

Week 8:   **Date** _____

_____ *chooses her words carefully.*

Do I need to exercise more control over the things I say? Do I often make a statement and then wish I hadn't? Do I think before I speak? How often do the things I say build up, encourage, or help other people, and how often do they foster negative or hurtful feelings?

Week 9:   **Date** _____

_____ *is respected by other people.*

How do other people view me? Do they trust me, feel they can count on me? Do they see me as someone they can learn from and whose views are worth considering? What could I do that would help me earn their respect?

Week 10:   **Date** _____

_____*'s children look up to her.*

What would I like my children to say about me years from now when they are adults and they look back on growing up under my guidance? What could I do today as a mother that might lay the groundwork for that kind of statement? Are the things I say and do worthy of my children's admiration? What changes could I make to be a better example for my children?

12 A WISE CHOICE

When I was in my early 20's, I went to visit my godmother, who had moved to another state. In the years since I had last seen her, she had been through some very trying personal difficulties, but had put her life back together and was thriving in her new home.

Naturally, we had a great deal of catching up to do. We talked about her experiences and mine, and about growth and change and adversity. We both made a number of philosophical observations about life's trials and triumphs.

After we had talked for a while she said, "You know, you're very wise for a person your age."

Now, I am realistic enough to suspect that her words were those of a loving godmother who could see only the best in the godchild she had watched grow up. Nevertheless, even now, in my moments of discouragement and low self-esteem, I like to pull her words out of my memory bank and savor the knowledge that at least one person thinks I am wise. It gives me the confidence to believe that I can solve the problem at hand, that surely I can come up with an answer. I love my godmother for many things, but I think I love her most of all for saying that to me (even if by some remote chance it might not be true.)

Wisdom is a precious commodity, and one that working mothers need in ample supply. We need wisdom to maintain those crucial balances we discussed in chapter 10. We need wisdom to make the numerous decisions we face every day, and to see past surface appearances into the hearts of people and situations. We need wisdom to manage the many relationships in our lives and to preserve a unified, focused sense of ourselves. We need wisdom to guide our children and prepare them for adulthood.

Our ideal working mother of Proverbs 31 is wise. The Bible devotes numerous verses to encouraging the pursuit of wisdom and describing its value. As our world grows more and more complex, wisdom becomes more and more essential to living a satisfying and balanced life instead of a confused and uncertain one. Above all, we need it to help us discern right choices from wrong ones.

What does it mean to you to be "wise"? Can you think of some friend, relative, or acquaintance you could point to and say "That is a wise person"? What would lead you to say that about him or her? How does the quality of wisdom reveal itself in a person's words and actions? Think about that for a moment, and then write your definition of wisdom here:

Wisdom is _____

_____.

For me, wisdom is largely the ability to distinguish what is real from what isn't and what is important from what isn't. That is admittedly a simplistic definition, but even after much thought, it's the best I can do. (Presumably you have come up with a better one!)

I'm not sure arriving at a dictionary definition of wisdom is essential anyway; I would rather explore the role it plays in our lives and, even more important, how we can increase our own wisdom.

Beyond the Limits

No matter how much education, skill, and experience we attain in our lives, the fact remains that human beings have limitations, and one of those is limited vision. We simply are not able to see or comprehend the totality of the universe. The concept of infinity is outside our mental reach; our minds can grasp, process, and store only a finite amount of information. As a result, we see only a limited portion of any situation. Our view of any problem or circumstance is colored by our relationship to it, by our past experience, and by our beliefs and values. As my mother puts it, "It's what you see from where you sit."

God, on the other hand, has unlimited vision. He sees the entire universe at a glance. He sees the past, the present, and the future. He sees inside our hearts and minds.

"Oh, the depth of the riches of the wisdom and knowledge of God!" wrote the apostle Paul (Romans 11:33). Wouldn't it be terrific if we could somehow tap into that infinite, all-seeing wisdom God has? Wouldn't that make it easier to find our way through the maze of decision-making each of us faces, instead of blundering along on our own limited knowledge and insight?

Here's some good news:

> *If any of you lacks wisdom, he should ask God,*
> *who gives generously to all without finding*
> *fault, and it will be given to him (James 1:5).*

God promises to give us wisdom if we only ask. Doesn't that make it seem silly to struggle along, tormented by uncertainty and confusion, when unlimited wisdom is ours for the asking?

Of course, when we ask God for wisdom, we enter into a problem-solving partnership with Him, a team effort to address the questions and choices in our lives. Entering into this partnership commits us to two major responsibilities:

1. When we ask God for wisdom, we must do so in the faith that we will receive it. In the business world, the art of negotiating has become a highly sophisticated game of move and countermove. Often the basic strategy involved is: Ask for pie-in-the-sky, and then work down from there. It's like the teenager who comes up to his mother and says, "Mom, can I go to the Bahamas for the weekend with my friends?" Naturally, his mother says no, so he aims lower: "Then can I have the car Saturday night?"

That approach isn't the one God wants us to use in seeking His wisdom. We aren't to enter into negotiations by asking for something we would never expect to receive. He wants us to ask, believing wholeheartedly that He'll respond.

2. We must be willing to be guided by His principles. When we enter into this problem-solving partnership with God, we are agreeing to play by His rules. If we ask God for wisdom, we must be willing to make decisions based on His standards of right and wrong, not on financial advantage, ego needs, convenience, popular opinion, what our friends think, or any of the many other forces that might pressure us to choose other options.

In this partnership, then, how does God give us wisdom? How do we tap into His wisdom to shape our decisions and perspectives?

Through Prayer

Prayer can help bring a problem into focus. When we ask God for guidance, we lay out the problem in prayer. As we do so, we put it into words in our own minds, which in itself is useful.

Putting a problem into words makes it seem more manageable; it becomes a concrete set of circumstances to deal with—however difficult dealing with it seems to be—rather than a frightening shadow lurking in the back of our minds. In virtually every kind of scientific research, corporate problem-solving, or strategic planning, the first step is to identify and state the problem. Prayer helps us do that.

In addition, prayer reassures us that we are not alone. By the very act of praying, we acknowledge that Someone whose wisdom is greater than ours is willing to share our burden of decision-making.

Through the Written Word

God ordered the universe, then He gave us guidelines for living in it. In the Bible He tells us the things we need to know to function effectively and to be the people He intends for us to be. "I am a stranger on earth," the psalmist wrote; "do not hide your commands from me" (119:19).

When we make decisions guided by God's instructions, we draw on His wisdom rather than relying completely on our own limited vision and insight. The Bible even cautions us to "lean not on your own understanding" (Proverbs 3:5).

Both the Old and New Testaments are filled with real people who had real decisions to make. The Bible is a storehouse of wisdom, written down for us in real-life terms.

Try this: Even if you are not a regular Bible reader, read the Book of Proverbs, starting at the beginning of chapter 10. Read a chapter or two a day for a week. As you read, consider the sound, down-to-earth advice those pithy little verses contain.

Then the next time you face a difficult decision, read those chapters again, a few at a time, and at the same time ask God to help you apply them to the decision at hand. Let yourself be encouraged and inspired as you draw on the wisdom that has served mankind for thousands of years and yet is as pertinent and practical today as when it was written.

Through Other People

Throughout my adult life, my friends have been an invaluable resource of wisdom and insight. I remember one episode in which I was very angry and frustrated over something that had not gone the way I thought it should. I went storming into my friend Chuck's office and told him about it.

"Well," he said, "what do you think you can learn from this?"

At the time, I was a little irritated with him for not being more sympathetic and commiserating with me in my anger and disappointment. As I cooled off, of course, I realized his question was a valuable one, and as I looked back on the incident I was able to learn an important lesson. Many times since then, in the wake of disappointing experiences, I have asked myself that same question: What can I learn from this?

Sometimes hearing about another person's painful experience or unwise decision can help us avoid making the same mistake. Sometimes our friends see things we don't see when we're too close to a situation. And sometimes an offhand observation by someone else can start us thinking in a new direction and lead to a fresh insight.

Through Example

What does wisdom look like in real life? Where can we find a person who exemplifies true wisdom?

In the New Testament. In Jesus, God showed us what His wisdom looks like in real life. Jesus was God's son, but He was human, too, and He struggled with hard choices and painful dilemmas just as we do.

Granted, Jesus was never a working mother—but He's still history's best role model for us. He was the consummation of personhood, the ultimate human being, who fully understood what it meant to be created in God's image and to live by God's laws. He was a patient listener, a loyal friend, an insightful teacher, a gentle care-giver—all those things we would like to be as we fulfill our many roles as working mothers. By looking to His example, we can catch a glimpse of His wisdom and learn how to cultivate that same wisdom for ourselves.

Do You Hear What I Hear?

Jesus was a listener. From the many biblical accounts of His interaction with people, we can picture Him listening intently, focusing on the speaker, not cutting the other person off or giving a hasty reply.

Just think how much we can learn from listening carefully to other people, listening not only to what they are saying aloud but also to the underlying feelings, needs, and messages. So often in our fast-paced lives, we mentally rush on to the next subject or give an answer while a person is still speaking, and we miss the real meaning of what they are saying.

Listening sounds like an easy enough skill to master. But how about this scenario?

You have had a rotten day at work, and you are coming down with a cold. You have just picked up your kids at the day-care center—late—and are now driving in peak traffic. How easy is it then to listen to your daughter's narration of how Bobby wrote Kimmie a note but Lewis took it and passed it to Jeffie, who read it and thought it was from Susie and he said Susie is a nerd and she started to cry and then the teacher asked why she was crying and she said because Jeffie called her a name so Jeffie got in trouble and then the teacher saw the note and she goes, "Who wrote this?" and Jeffie goes, "It wasn't me," and Susie just keeps crying, and...

See? Listening isn't quite as easy as it seems. But it's a key to learning what is going on in the lives, hearts, and minds of the people around us. If we could learn to be more patient and effective listeners, I believe we would take a major step toward greater wisdom.

As we look at Jesus as a listener, we need to bear in mind that He listened to God, too. God promises to give us wisdom if we ask—but we have to be listening when He answers.

Based on My Observations...

The young police officer was scrupulously polite as he wrote out a speeding ticket with my name on it, but that didn't relieve my embarrassment and anger with myself. He had stopped me for going 42 miles an hour in a 30 m.p.h. zone—in my own neighborhood. I felt humiliated by my lack of observation. How could I have missed the sign that changed the speed limit from 40 to 30?

We have so much on our minds at any given moment that it is very easy to fail to notice what is going on around us—like when there's a change in the speed limit. Being preoccupied is an occupational hazard of being a working mother. Some days I can almost see a computer readout in my brain saying, "Insufficient memory... Insufficient memory...."

It's expensive and embarrassing to miss a speed-limit sign. But when we get too out of touch with what's happening around us, we run the risk of missing something truly important. I think a prerequisite of wisdom is being observant about our environment.

Jesus was in touch with what was going on around Him. He repeatedly used examples from the everyday world to convey important spiritual truths. He compared faith to a tiny seed, or to building a house on rock instead of sand. He described faultfinding as looking at the speck of dirt in another person's eye while ignoring the plank in our own. He compared God's kingdom to finding a valuable pearl, laboring in a vineyard, or planting a crop. He observed the world around Him and used those observations to help people understand His message.

He observed people, too. He could readily see who was sincere and who was phony. He could tell whose heart was open to truth and whose was selfish and hard. The local religious leaders' attempts to deceive Him failed because He saw through their seemingly innocent questions. He met a Samaritan woman and instantly knew how desperately she wanted someone to love her and tell her she was a person of worth. And when a rich young man asked Him how to get into heaven, Jesus immediately saw that the man's wealth was an obstacle to his spiritual growth.

The Bible tells us people were amazed at Jesus' teachings. You and I may not dazzle anyone with our wisdom, but we can certainly follow Jesus' example by being keen observers of people, events, and situations around us.

Surely a part of wisdom is the ability to understand the meaning of what happens in our world. In order to understand it, we have to observe it first.

It's in the Book

A friend and I were talking recently about violence on TV and in movies. I said I believed that seeing violence in the media made it seem acceptable to young people and that it was probably a bad influence on them. He said he had read, on the other hand, that psychologists believe media violence enables people to "act out" their own violent tendencies in a harmless, fantasy-like way, which, in turn, may prevent them from actually committing acts of violence.

I don't know which of these views is right. I suspect in a few years another study of media violence will come out and present totally different conclusions. That's the trouble with contemporary "wisdom": It changes. The people who believed the earth was flat were surely considered wise at the time—until someone proved it wasn't. There were people in our own century who believed that Hitler's slaughter of millions of Jews was "right." There are experts today who tell us children need strict discipline, and also those who tell us to be lenient. Some people say "Be a pal to your child" while others say "Maintain your authority." It's a philosophical jungle out there.

The next generation's trendsetters will have a whole different set of ideas for rearing children, dealing with social and moral issues, and maintaining the balance of world power. If we pursue wisdom that reflects the current popular philosophy, we will be chasing a slippery quarry indeed!

> *See to it that no one takes you captive through hollow and deceptive philosophy, which depends on human tradition and the basic principles of this world rather than on Christ (Colossians 2:8).*

That brings us to the most important characteristic of Jesus' wisdom: It was centered on God's commandments. Jesus listened; He observed; and then He interpreted the things He saw and heard in light of the fundamental truths He knew. When Jesus faced choices, He didn't have to check out the latest philosophical writings or see which way the wind of popular opinion was blowing. He had only to base His choices and His actions on God's laws, which never change.

If we truly want to be wise—and working mothers certainly need to be—I believe that we, too, must anchor our wisdom in those principles which have served seekers of wisdom well for thousands of years. And God offers us an inexhaustible source of timeless wisdom just for the asking.

> *Therefore everyone who hears these words of mine and puts them into practice is like a wise man who built his house on the rock. The rain came down, the streams rose, and the winds blew and beat against that house; yet it did not fall, because it had its foundation on the rock. But everyone who hears these words of mine and does not put them into practice is like a foolish man who built his house on sand. The rain came down, the streams rose,and the winds blew and beat against that house, and it fell with a great crash.*
>
> *When Jesus had finished saying these things, the crowds were amazed at his teaching...*
> *(Matthew 7:24-28).*

Other Good
Harvest House Reading

THE THINKING CHRISTIAN WOMAN
Taking Responsibility for Your Own Spiritual Growth
by *Helen Hosier*

Time-consuming needs of everyday living leave a woman little time to nourish her relationship with God. But there's no more important need in the life of every Christian woman than taking time to develop biblically based thinking in order to apply the principles of God's Word to her daily life. Learning how to bring the very thoughts of God into the urgent needs of the day will help every woman: • Handle her emotions intelligently • Take charge of health, finances, and personal development • Discover the lasting benefits of solitude and study of the Bible • Develop a conquering spirit • Live life with a renewed heart and a joyful mind • Find times of rest and refreshment. Valuable help for today's busy woman.

EATING RIGHT!
by *Emilie Barnes* and *Sue Gregg*

Confused by one fad diet after another and the conflicting advice from nutritionists about what to eat? Bestselling author Emilie Barnes and Sue Gregg approach the conflicts involved in food selection, preparation, and kitchen organization with practical help and a *realistic* approach based on common-sense guidelines and God's plan for healthy eating. Develop an "eating lifestyle" that really works!

THE QUIET HEART
by *June Masters Bacher*

In this all-new devotional by June Masters Bacher, each daily devotional begins with a suggested Scripture reading, and through anecdotes, poetry, and prayer inspires each reader to see life with a fresh perspective. A day-by-day "friend" that encourages a quiet heart so you can come to know God and learn how much richer knowing Him makes each day.

QUIET MOMENTS FOR WOMEN
by *June Masters Bacher*

Though written for women, this devotional will benefit the entire family. Mrs. Bacher's down-to-earth, often humorous experiences have a daily message of God's love for you!

SURVIVAL FOR BUSY WOMEN
Establishing Efficient Home Management
by *Emilie Barnes*

A hands-on manual for establishing a more efficient home-management program. Over 25 charts and forms can be personalized to help you organize your home.

LITTLE TALKS ABOUT GOD AND YOU
by *V. Gilbert Beers*

If you're wondering what to do for family devotions, now is the time to stop wondering and start reading *Little Talks About God and You*. Illustrated on every page, each little talk includes a small story to illustrate a Bible truth, questions to share with your child, a Bible reading, and a prayer. These little talks will lead you and your child through a refreshing, fun-filled exploration of life. Gil Beers, past editor of *Christianity Today*, is well known for his children's literature. Illustrated.

BEDTIME HUGS FOR LITTLE ONES
by *Debby Boone*

Written for children ages two to six, *Bedtime Hugs* is a unique collaboration by recording star and actress Debby Boone and her artist husband, Gabriel Ferrer. A collection of bedtime stories about many of the things children think about—growing up, dreams, the dark, shooting stars, being loved—it's written in a style that provides parents and children a rich opportunity to talk and share during the bedtime story hour. The musical focus of Debby's life is aptly reflected in the lyrical style of her imaginative writing, and Gabri turns favorite childhood images into vibrant and whimsical illustrations. This storybook will be a favorite of parents and children alike.

Dear Reader:

We would appreciate hearing from you regarding this Harvest House nonfiction book. It will enable us to continue to give you the best in Christian publishing.

1. What most influenced you to purchase *The Working Mother's Guide to Sanity*?
   - ☐ Author
   - ☐ Subject matter
   - ☐ Backcover copy
   - ☐ Recommendations
   - ☐ Cover/Title
   - ☐ _____

2. Where did you purchase this book?
   - ☐ Christian bookstore
   - ☐ General bookstore
   - ☐ Department store
   - ☐ Grocery store
   - ☐ Other

3. Your overall rating of this book:
   ☐ Excellent   ☐ Very good   ☐ Good   ☐ Fair   ☐ Poor

4. How likely would you be to purchase other books by this author?
   - ☐ Very likely
   - ☐ Somewhat likely
   - ☐ Not very likely
   - ☐ Not at all

5. What types of books most interest you?
   (check all that apply)
   - ☐ Women's Books
   - ☐ Marriage Books
   - ☐ Current Issues
   - ☐ Self Help/Psychology
   - ☐ Bible Studies
   - ☐ Fiction
   - ☐ Biographies
   - ☐ Children's Books
   - ☐ Youth Books
   - ☐ Other _____

6. Please check the box next to your age group.
   - ☐ Under 18
   - ☐ 18-24
   - ☐ 25-34
   - ☐ 35-44
   - ☐ 45-54
   - ☐ 55 and over

Mail to: Editorial Director
Harvest House Publishers
1075 Arrowsmith
Eugene, OR 97402

Name _____

Address _____

City _____ State _____ Zip _____

Thank you for helping us to help you in future publications!